CONSCIENCE

Conscience

by Spiros Zodhiates, Th.D.

**An exegetical exposition of
Luke 11:33-36 from the Greek text**

AMG
PUBLISHERS

COPYRIGHT 1982 BY SPIROS ZODHIATES
PRINTED IN THE UNITED STATES OF AMERICA
ALL RIGHTS RESERVED
ISBN 0-89957-555-2
LIBRARY OF CONGRESS 82-71843
SECOND PRINTING 1986

Cover Design: Florence Anderson
Cover photograph taken in Covenant College Chapel,
Chattanooga, Tennessee

AMG PUBLISHERS CHATTANOOGA, TN 37421

Dedicated to
my faithful co-workers of over thirty years
Don and Louise Ebner
in whose conscience Jesus reigns
in His full light and splendor.

PREFACE

How important are your eyes? They are just like a lamp. But are they? The lamp gives light whereas the eye receives light. Why then did the Lord equate the eye to a lamp? You will find out as you read these pages. There is more to it than first meets the eye!

How can the light that is in us become darkness? The Lord Jesus in Luke 11:33 through 36 spoke about man's conscience — that is his light. But He also told us that such a light can become darkness. And then what?

How about the dark spots on our conscience? Is it possible for a Christian to have dark spots in his life? What are they? How can they be lightened? Jesus desires His light to fill our hearts without any darkness. It is possible. This study will help you find out and realize it in and through the enablement of the Holy Spirit.

Spiros Zodhiates

Chattanooga, TN
November 2, 1981

CONTENTS

1

The Parable of the Candle

In Luke 11:33-36, our Lord says: "No man, when he hath lighted a candle, putteth it in a secret place, neither under a bushel, but on a candlestick, that they which come in may see the light. The light of the body is the eye; therefore when thine eye is single, thy whole body also is full of light; but when thine eye is evil, thy body also is full of darkness. Take heed therefore that the light which is in thee be not darkness. If thy whole body therefore be full of light, having no part dark, the whole shall be full of light, as when the bright shining of a candle doth give thee light."

No one can doubt that this constitutes one of the most searching teachings of the Lord Jesus Christ. This parable occurs in three other passages in the Synoptic Gospels. We find it in Mark 4:21 very briefly: "Is a candle brought to be put under a bushel, or under a bed, and not to be set on a candlestick?" And then in Luke 8:16 we read, "No man, when he hath lighted a candle, covereth it with a vessel, or putteth it under a bed; but setteth it on a candlestick, that they which enter in may see the light." And in Matthew 5:15, which is part of the Sermon on the Mount, we read these words: "Neither do men light a candle, and put it under a bushel, but on a candlestick; and it giveth light unto all that are in the house."

What is the proposition that our Lord is setting forth? The one use and purpose of a candle, He declares, is to enable those who come into a room to see by its light. It is silly to light a candle and then put a vessel like a peck measure (actually that is the literal meaning of the word in the Greek text) over it, or to put the candle in a cellar where its light would serve no one, and leave the people in the room above in the dark.

A Teaching Whose Depths Can Never Be Fully Plumbed

These various statements in Mark, Luke, and Matthew were undoubtedly made at different times. This was a repeated teaching of our Lord concerning the light, that the eye was the instrument through which the whole body is illuminated. Here in Luke 11:33-36 we have the fullest statement of this teaching. Though it is worded so simply, we can never expect fully to fathom the depth of its meaning and suggestion. No one can read our Lord's words without being conscious of a meaning in them that is difficult to grasp and define. There is a touch of mysticism in them. Though they are found in the Gospel of Luke, and substantially also in the Gospel of Matthew, they sound like an extract from the Gospel of John.

If we look back to the preceding context, verses 29-32 of Luke 11, we find that the Lord has been reproaching the Israelites of His day as an evil and adulterous generation, because, though they had a perpetual witness for God in their own hearts, they did not listen to it. And though in Christ they had the greatest of all proofs that God was with them, they did not recognize the manifestation of God in Him but were greedy for more and greater wonders, as signs of an omnipotent and irresistible power. They were evil, because it is only evil that obliterates or obscures the true and perpetual sign, the sign in the conscience. And they were adulterous because there is a certain impurity in the appeal of a heart for more proofs of God's presence and power, when a person does not really want to see God and to share in His holiness.

The Israelites Blind to the Light of the World

Yet evil and adulterous as they are, a sign such as they demand has been given them, a sign greater than that which convinced the Queen of Sheba that Solomon was taught of God, and greater than that which convinced the men of Nineveh that Jonah was sent to reveal the righteous judgment of God against all unrighteousness in men. One was with them, and had long been with them, who was greater than Solomon, greater than Jonah, wiser than the wisest sage, more righteous than any prophet or teacher of righteousness. The Son of man was the great light of the world and yet they could not see it. They were blind. They were an evil and adulterous generation. And if you cannot see truth, don't blame truth. If you cannot see Jesus Christ in all His glory, don't blame Him, blame yourself.

Jonah's Unwillingness and Christ's Immediate Obedience Contrasted

Now Jonah was unwilling to go where God asked him to go originally. And God dealt with him. But here the Lord Jesus Christ did not shirk the duty that He came to perform. Yes, at one time He prayed to His Father that, if it were His will He would remove the cup, but He said, "Not my will, but

13

thine, be done" (Luke 22:42). The Lord Jesus Christ was greater than Jonah because, although He could escape the cross for His own good, He did not do it. And these evil and adulterous people could not see the superiority of the Lord Jesus Christ to Jonah.

Are you reluctant to go where God once asked you to go? Jesus was not. And sometimes, when you demonstrate the courage that the Lord Jesus Christ demonstrated, it is also possible that people will not see how brightly you shine in God's sight. But don't be discouraged. The Lord Jesus said to those who rejected Him that it was not His fault but theirs. It was because their eye was evil that they could not see Him as the light of the world, a greater than Jonah.

Did the Lord ever deal with you by casting you into the sea because of your disobedience to Him? But symbolically something like that can happen to any disobedient servant of God. Examine your adversities, lest they be God-ordained. It was God who caused Jonah to suffer because of his disobedience. Jesus Christ was greater than Jonah in that He did not disobey God, and yet these people of His own generation could not see the greatness of Christ's obedience unto death.

We, Too, May Be Unrecognized in Our Service for Christ

One of the things that really disturbs us is that, when we live in a generation as sinful, as adulterous, as evil, as the one that Jesus lived in, though our willingness to do the will of God and to live for Christ is manifest, nobody recognizes our sacrifices for Him. We may be greater than Jonah, even as the Lord Jesus was, but He went unrecognized, and so may we. The brightness of His glory was not seen, because the eyes of the people were dim.

When the spirit of obedience finally came to Jonah, God

demonstrated His power. You know, it is a marvel how God deals with us. He often gives us a second and a third and a fourth chance to do that which He originally asked us to do. But the Lord Jesus Christ went to the cross the first time, immediately. He set His face resolutely toward Jerusalem, yet instead of recognizing how willing He was to do the will of His Father for their sakes, these people rejected Him.

Jonah went to Nineveh knowing full well that the people were sinful there, but he didn't go immediately. He wanted to escape that responsibility. The Lord Jesus Christ also knew how evil and adulterous His generation was, and yet He went to the cross immediately. Jesus did not give up, nor should we, whether our willingness to sacrifice, to obey, to go where God wants us to go and to do what God wants us to do is recognized by others or not. Jesus was not recognized in His greatness, not because of any fault of His own, but because of the blindness of the people.

To See God, One's Inner Eye Must Be Attuned to Receive His Light

Do you recognize the Lord Jesus for all that He is in your life? "The light of the body is the eye: therefore when thine eye is single, thy whole body also is full of light; but when thine eye is evil, thy body also is full of darkness." It is because the eyes of people are evil that their whole being is in darkness. For the reception of this light, as of all light, there must be a corresponding organ capable of perceiving it — a single or healthy eye, an open eye that desires the light.

What did the Lord mean by the eye being single? He did not say the eye is the light of the body but the lamp of the body. If there is no light the eye is useless. The light is not in the eye, but outside it and independent of it. The eye receives, interprets and applies the light. The eye then

15

regulates the motions of the body. The eye sees because light is shining.

SINGLE EYE EX PLAINED ⤵

Then our Lord said that the eye can be either single or evil. But the opposite of evil is good, not single. Why did the Lord use "single" as the desired condition of the eye? The Greek word for single is *haplous* which means single-folded, without a fold. *Tetraplous* would mean four-folds or four-folded. If the eye has folds in it, it's diseased, it cannot see correctly. If your eye is not *haplous,* single, it is *astigmatic* or it suffers from astigmatism. That is a condition of the eye in which rays of light do not converge to a point in the retina. That means there is some fold there, something out of place, something complicated. The eye is not single. The eye that does not suffer from astigmatism, that is single, not folded over, can see things clearly and the whole body is properly lighted and guided. The eye then is the proper lamp to guide the body.

The opposite of the single eye is the evil eye, according to our Lord. The Greek word for evil is *poneeros,* which means not only evil in itself but also in its influence. Your eye if not single, healthy, is diseased. But its disease, evil, does not stop with itself. It affects the whole body. It will lead it astray. It will make you see double. It will give you the wrong impression of others. The eye regulates the body. But if the eye will give to the body the wrong vision of things and persons, it will lead it to do those things that it ought not to. A diseased eye will lead a body in darkness or where it ought not to be. The proof that those to whom the Lord Jesus was speaking lacked such an eye was that they were still asking for signs when the supreme sign, the Light of the world, stood before them, and they would not perceive it.

To ask a sign of Christ was as though a man should go to the sun shining at noonday and ask for a lamp to guide his feet through the darkness. They were blind. Had these people possessed a single and open eye they would have recognized the light of the world in Christ far more easily than the Queen of Sheba recognized the wisdom of God in Solomon, or than the Ninevites recognized the voice of God's righteousness in the warning of Jonah. The mere fact that they did not see light in the Lord Jesus Christ, who was the light, was sufficient and damning proof that their eye was evil. As predicted in Isaiah 6:9, and variously quoted in Matthew 13:14, Mark 4:12, and Acts 28:26, "seeing they saw, and did not perceive; hearing they heard and did not understand."

How foolish it would be for me, for instance, to go into a room and say, "You tell me there are audio and video waves in here; you must be crazy. I can't hear them. I can't see them."

"Oh," you say, "Wait. I'll prove it to you." You turn on the radio and tune it to a station, and out comes the sound of voices. You turn on the television set and tune it to a station and pictures appear. Now, I was right in saying I could not see or hear the video and audio waves. It was because I did not tune in on the proper instrument.

If I want to see the light, I must use my inner eye, but that eye must be healthy; as the Lord Jesus Christ said, it must be single. My eye must be tuned to the proper transmitter in order to become the receiver of the light of God. I must set my heart in tune with God if I want to hear His voice, and to see Him in His glory.

It is impossible for us to see God without permitting our spirit to be tuned to the Spirit of God. It was impossible for these unbelieving Israelites to see in Jesus Christ a greater than Solomon, a greater than Jonah, to see Him as the Savior of the world.

THINK IT OVER

1. What character trait prominent in Jesus Christ, and lacking in Jonah, does God value most highly in His servants? (See I Sam. 15:22.) OBEDIENCE

2. What faculty in us may rightly be designated "the eye of the soul?" (See Titus 1:15.) CONSCIENCE

3. In what sense were the Israelites "evil," and in what sense "adulterous," in the estimation of Jesus Christ?

Pg 13 FIRST PARAGRAPH!

TEACh

2

Opening Our Eyes to the Light

Another meaning that is suggested by Luke 11:33-36 is that as Jonah was a sign unto the Ninevites so also shall the Son of man be to this generation. Now Jonah was a sign to the men of Nineveh, not only in that he spoke to them in words that quickened and aroused their consciences, but also in that, in all probability, he told them how he had been for three days buried in the depths of the sea, and yet had been delivered from death, that he might bring them God's call to repentance.

And our Lord in like manner, after speaking to His countrymen in a way to arouse and alarm their consciences, foretells that He too must be buried and yet rise again from the dead to bring them to repentance. So familiar is this fact to Him, so clearly does He foresee His future death and resurrection while yet He is in the full vigor of His life and ministry, that He can speak of it almost casually, half hiding it and half revealing it in the simple parable of the candle. He is the light of the world, the great light of life. In referring to the sign of Jonah He spoke of His coming death and resurrection. And when this actually came to pass, the same people continued to be unbelievers. They could not see deity in that man, the Lord Jesus, who walked among them.

Can you see all that there is in Jesus Christ? He's there, but perhaps your eyes are dim. Ask the Holy Spirit to open them, that you may see "the glory of God in the face of Jesus Christ" (II Cor. 4:6).

Yet, even then, when Jesus Christ has reappeared from and dissipated the night of death, only those will be able to see and to walk in His light whose eyes have been exercised and trained to discern the true Lord and Ruler of men. And the more wisely exercised, the more finely trained their eyes have been, the more will they see in Him, the more fully will they behold and reflect His glory.

It is the person, for instance, who has been trained in art appreciation who can fully appreciate great works of art. An untrained eye may look at a beautiful statue or painting and see only the commonplace. This is what these people considered our Lord, a commonplace man. They did not attribute to Him the glory that belonged to Him.

Only a Clear and Healthy Eye Can Fully See Light in the Physical World

After referring to Himself as the light and life of men, our Lord goes on to say that, for the apprehension of light, a corresponding and appropriate organ is required. This organ is the eye. The eye that receives light for the whole body gives light to the whole body — the light in which all its activities are carried on — and may therefore be called the lamp or candle of the body. But the amount of light received and distributed depends on the power and accuracy of the eye that receives it. The organ may be diseased. It may prevent the access of

20

the light or pervert it so that we do not see things as they are, or even in extreme cases do not see them at all. If this solitary candle is put out, how profound must be the darkness in which we walk! If it is obscured or distorted, how radical and misleading must be the errors into which it betrays us. It is of the utmost importance, therefore, that we should keep the one organ which receives and imparts light — the light of all our seeing, all our working, all our progress — in a healthy condition. It is of the gravest necessity that we should seek to remedy and correct every defect in it, that we should raise it to its highest power and train it to the most accurate and delicate discriminations. No candle is kindled that it may be hidden, whether wholly as in a cellar beneath the room we occupy, or partially as under a bed in the room, and least of all the lamp of the body which alone makes all other light visible to us and useful. That is quite plain and clear.

Only a Healthy "Inner Eye" Can See Spiritual Truth

In all this we have been dealing only with a form of the passage of Luke 11:33-36, only with its outside parable. For while speaking of the eye of the body, it is obvious that it was the eye of the soul that our Lord had in mind. The spiritual part in us has its perceptive faculty as well as the physical part, and it is even more important that the spiritual candle should be lifted to its due place and kept burning brightly than that the physical candle should be placed on the lampstand and not hidden in a cellar or under a bushel basket.

If then we turn from the form of the passage to its substance, what is it that our Lord is teaching us in these words? I believe He is saying that a healthy, trained, unprejudiced understanding is required for the due apprehension and appreciation of spiritual truth, and that the health and power of the understanding by which we receive and impart

21

the truth depends mainly on the establishing of right attitudes toward the hearing and sifting of God's Word as revealed in the Scriptures. A desire to know and follow the truth at whatever cost is a prerequisite to "seeing" the truth.

Inward Light Always Results in an Outward Manifestation of Christ's Indwelling

Furthermore, I take Him to mean that in proportion as this inward perc   n and love of the truth grows pure and strong within u   'r whole outward life will reflect the power of that truth, and   ʃ inward light will penetrate and irradiate all our external actions, till it shines through and transfigures the whole person.

Remember, it is of the capacity for interpreting the signs of a divine presence and activity that the Lord Jesus Christ is speaking. He Himself, He says, is the greatest of all signs that God is with men. If the Israelites had not been wholly blind, blinder than the Gentiles who came from the uttermost parts of the earth to hear the wisdom of Solomon, or who listened and repented at the preaching of Jonah, they must have recognized the presence, the wisdom, and the righteousness of God in Him. That they did not was a sufficient and damning proof that their faculty of spiritual perception, their power to receive and radiate the light of truth, was corrupted, distorted, diseased.

What Causes Impairment of Spiritual Eyesight?

Now what causes the impairment of our spiritual eyesight? This disease to the eyes of the people annulled their power of true intellectual perception. It sprang, as we may infer from Matthew 6:22, 23, from the evil and perverted affections of their hearts. Matthew reports Christ as teaching men that where their treasure is there their heart will be also, and then as going on to say, "The light of the body is the eye: if therefore thine eye be single, thy whole body shall be full of light. But if thine eye be evil, thy whole body shall be full of darkness." And from the connection in which the words stand it is clear that He means to suggest that the eye of the soul is affected by the condition of the heart, that our affections limit and determine our perceptions, that men fail to see what they do not want to see, and are able to see what they care to see, what they are looking for because they love it.

The Ability to See and Reflect the Light of God's Revelation Depends on Our Willingness to Receive It

Even as a general truth, this thought is confirmed by our common experience. For we all know that men are slow to see what they are reluctant to see, that they may even blind themselves, at least for a time, to truths that condemn courses of action on which they are strongly bent. But it is the special application of this general truth which Christ had in view that we must bear in mind. And this special application was that, when God is revealing Himself to men, whether in the wisdom of the wise, or the reproofs of the holy, or even in the perfect wisdom and unblemished holiness of the Son of man, this power of receiving and reflecting the light of that revelation depends mainly on their willingness to receive it, on their freedom from the passions and affections which prejudice the mind against the truth of God which lead them to hate and resent the light that condemns them.

Now is not that true to our experience, true to the experience of every man in every day? What will happen if we take the highest forms of spiritual truth to men who are plunged in sensuality, or who are living only for the things of time, or who are devoted to aims that can only be reached unrighteously, or to men to whom their own private and

23

selfish ends are of paramount interest and importance? Can they recognize and respond to the beauty, the truth, and the irresistible attractiveness of the truth, to the righteousness, the life, the love we place before them? Will they see God in it, a manifestation of the supreme good, a disclosure of the true ideal and the true aims of human life? Will they not rather blink before the momentary irradiation, close their eyes to it, return to the dark and tortuous paths in which we found them walking, and perhaps even turn again and rend us for having disturbed them in their sordid pursuits even for an instant?

Cannot even good men close their eyes to the facts and discoveries of science if they do not want to see them, if they fear that to receive them would be to disturb the accepted and comfortable beliefs in which they have been cradled? Cannot even men of science close their eyes to the evidences of immoral and immortal spirit in man, or to the signs which indicate the presence and activity of God, whether in nature or in history, if they are bent on reducing all the phenomena of the universe under their own materialistic conceptions of order and law? The eye sees only what it brings in itself, power to see. Its power of seeing depends on the aims men cherish, on the courses they have chosen.

The Danger of Closing Our Eyes to the Light

Almost every sensitive and thoughtful man, even though he has no formulated religion, is haunted at times by that sense of an unseen but all-encompassing presence which the ancient psalmist of Israel has so perceptively rendered for us in Psalm 139. And yet we are all conscious also that at times this power retires from us, so to speak, leaves us to choose our own course, and watches to see what we will do when we are thus left free. Who does not know that at such times, yes, and at all times, we may disregard that presence, harden

24

ourselves against that all-encompassing power, close our eyes against the light too great and pure and piercing for our weak, sin-burdened hearts, until we become blind to it, or plunge into open rebellion against it? May God help us not to close our eyes to such dazzling truth as Christ presents to all men, and reject it as insufficient proof of His claims.

How Will God Judge People in Regard to the Light He Gives Them?

There's a great deal of confusion and misapprehension today as to how God is going to judge people. Will it be by the light which they have had or by their reception of that light? I believe it is the latter. God has a way of bringing the witness of His Spirit to all people, but not all people receive it in the same manner. God's revelation is constant to the world. It is supplemented in many ways. God is ever seeking to disclose Himself to us, to come into vital and quickening contact with some part of our manifold nature. It is not merely that He wants us to know Him and believe some facts or truths about Him. He wants to give Himself to us, and not mere notions and beliefs about Himself. He woos us by the slow and gradual processes of His providence, by the discipline of sorrow and joy, by the experience and examples of our immediate neighbors, by inspirations addressed to the seeking intellect of the philosopher, to the yearning imagination of the poet, to the common reason and conscience of all men. God speaks to us by the biographies He has moved holy men to write, by writing out the history of one nation, Israel, in full, with a constant eye to its relation to truth and righteousness; and above all by the incarnation of all truth and righteousness and love in the perfect life of the Lord Jesus Christ. He has endeavored to penetrate the mists that dim our vision of Him, to draw the veil and to purge away the disease which impairs

25

or obstructs our view of Him. You could comprehend the full meaning of John 1:9 if you could read it in the Greek text. "He was the light always [i.e., He has always been the light], the true One which lights." *Phootizoo* is the Greek word. He gives light constantly. This light illumines every man coming into the world. In other words, there isn't a single individual that one day can stand before God truthfully and say, "I had no light shine upon me," no more than he could stand and truthfully say that the light of the sun has not shone upon him. Impossible. Each person receives or rejects that light, but no person can claim that the light has never shone.

There Is Always Light for Those Who Have Eyes to See

In all these ways, then, and in many more, God is seeking us, seeking to show and to impart Himself to us. There is no lack of light. From a thousand different centers the primal and eternal light is shining all around us. What we lack, if as yet we do not see God, is not light to see Him by, but an eye to see Him with. And if the eye is blind, so that we cannot see Him, or distorted and diseased so that we do not see Him as He is, that is because our hearts are so preoccupied with other affections and pursuits that we do not care to see Him.

Would it not be worth the trouble to lift our eyes to heaven and open them to the light? Many a man may sing in church, "Teach me, my God and King, in all things Thee to see, and what I do in anything to do it as to Thee," who would nevertheless be more than a little startled were he to see God by his own fireside or in his own office or factory (where nevertheless God as surely is), watching to see whether he did for God what he knew God required in the home, in the shop, or amid the excitements of a contested election. By our defective vision of God's universal presence and activity, we

26

fall short of our proper and highest blessedness.

The Transfiguring Power of the Inward Light

There is a wonderful splendor in the words with which our Lord closes this remarkable passage of Luke 11:33-36. He would have us use and train the eye of the soul, keep the candle always on the stand, because in proportion as we cherish this inward light all things will become full of light for us. And we ourselves will be transfigured by the power of the inward light shining outwards, because our whole nature will be transparent to and irradiated with a heavenly glory. For as we kindle and tend this lamp of the soul, our whole nature becomes clear, purer, transparent, till at last we stand full in the bright shining of the Son, the very light of heaven.

And what is all this but saying that we are to let our inward light prove and approve itself by our good works, as Matthew 5:16 tells us, that men seeing our good deeds may glorify our Father who is in heaven by a life as bright and good as Christ's own.

Let us then open our eyes to the light, that is to say, open our hearts to the God who is always seeking us and disclosing Himself to us. Let us suffer the sacred influence we received from Him to radiate, to shine forth on others, through the good deeds of a life at one with His will, and in the end we shall become radiant with God, transparent to God. His rays will shine clean through us, through every part of our nature. We shall not only see Him but share in the full splendor of His everlasting glory.

THINK IT OVER

1. Describe the similarity between Jonah's "sign" to his generation, and our Lord's "sign" to the people of Israel in His day.
2. What causes impairment of spiritual eyesight? What limits our perception of truth?
3. Will God judge people according to the light they have been given, or according to how they respond to that light?
4. What transfiguration of your personal attitudes and actions has God's light brought about in your life? Check the following:

      _____ My obedience to His will as set forth in His Word has increased.

      _____ My disposition in the home, at work, or school has improved.

      _____ I seek to witness by word and deed to Christ's saving grace.

   (Note: these are just a few of the transformations that the light can bring about.)

3

Christianity — A Religion of Light

Light is a synonym of all that is beautiful and glorious in the universe of God, whether in the material or in the spiritual realm. Perhaps the most magnificent declaration ever uttered is that recorded in the book of Genesis by Moses: "God said, Let there be light: and there was light" (Gen. 1:3). Light is the most perfect emblem of purity we can imagine. We cannot conceive of the possibility of its defilement. Light is the source of beauty; we could have no concept of beauty without it. The colors of the rainbow, the endlessly varied and pleasing pictures portrayed before us in the flowers, the ever-changing shades in sky or forest, the delicate tints in the plumage of the bird, the flush of health on the human cheek, the glory of the sunrise, the splendor of the sunset — all these and ten thousand other manifestations of beauty are creatures of the light.

Thank God for Sight — His Free Gift to All

Light is not only beautiful in itself, is not only the source of

29

beauty, it is the free gift of God. Sometimes a person may complain, "There isn't anything God has given me for which I should thank Him." But wait a minute. What about light, the free gift of God to all, the common grace of God? Where would we be, if it were not for God giving light, yes, external light to everybody who comes into the world? (Yes, some are born blind, yet they reap many benefits from the light of the sun.) All the wealth of the goldfields could not purchase an added moment's sunshine on any single day.

Light, furthermore, is the single source of fruitfulness. Every time you eat some fruit, realize that it is the result of the light given by God. The life and beauty of the world never could have come to pass without light. You sometimes feel you have nothing to thank God for? Thank Him for light. The flowers bloom, the trees wave their branches, the grass carpets the earth, the flocks and herds cover the hillsides, the fields of grain glisten in the sun, the birds form themselves into choirs, and mankind develops and prospers and goes forth with courage to occupy the earth and possess it in the lands of light. This world would speedily become a lifeless globe without light. Light sustains fertility and life. You and I couldn't live a moment without it.

Christianity — A Religion of Light

The religion of the Lord Jesus Christ is a religion of light. One of the most splendid descriptions of our Heavenly Father is in the words of John: "God is light, and in him is no darkness at all" (I John 1:5). James says, "Every good gift and every perfect gift is from above, and cometh down from the Father of lights" (James 1:17). Note James' descriptive name for God, "the Father of lights." And the Lord Jesus declares that those who seek to do the will of God are the "children of light" (John 12:36). Our Savior never said a more splendid thing about Himself than when He uttered that sublime declaration, "I am the light of the world" (John 8:12 and 9:5). Everywhere in the Scriptures, light is used as an emblem of the righteous character of those who are the true children of God. Yes, the religion of the Lord Jesus Christ is a religion of light.

Light a Symbol of Joy and Hope

Light is also used to symbolize the gladness and the certain hope which shall be the inspiration and reward of such a character. The Psalmist says, "Light is sown for the righteous, and gladness for the upright in heart" (Ps. 97:11). And again it is confidently declared, "Unto the upright there ariseth light in the darkness " (Ps. 112:4). And the blessed promise is made to all those who walk the way of faithfulness that even though they draw near to the valley of the shadow of death, they shall not be surrounded by darkness, for "at evening time it shall be light" (Zech. 14:7). Again the Word says, "The path of the just is like the shining light, that shineth more and more unto the perfect day" (Prov. 4:18).

God's Gift of an Enlightened Conscience

But it isn't just an outer light that comes to us which is the source of beauty, fruitfulness, and the free gift of God to all, but God also gives an inner light. Let's consider this inner light of the conscience as it is strengthened and made perfect by the Word of God and the presence of the Holy Spirit. God has put His light in our hearts. The Scriptures declare, "The spirit of man is the candle of the Lord" (Prov. 20:27). All souls are illuminated, more or less, by the heavenly shining. No man or woman anywhere in the world has been left entirely in the dark. The conscience shining more or less brightly, though it sometimes seems only like the smoking flax, is a

31

light from heaven in every human soul.

But conscience is not a perfect guide; therefore God has given us His Word and the Holy Comforter, who is sent to all hearts that will receive Him, to enlighten our minds and to reveal the will of God to our hearts. It is not enough to be conscientious, but we are required to bring to the education of our conscience the Word of God and the aid of the Holy Spirit. Many very wrong and evil things that have brought and do bring great sorrow and disaster to the world have been done in the past and are being done today by conscientious people.

Physical and Spiritual Colorblindness

Colorblindness, especially in its bearing upon the efficiency of railroad men, is well known. It has been found by careful investigation that from two to three hundred persons in every one thousand are unable to distinguish clearly one color from another. They are colorblind. This becomes, of course, a life and death matter in the handling of railway trains, inasmuch as the danger signal on railroad tracks is a red light. This was especially dangerous in an earlier day, when they had to have guards to open the gates at railroad crossings. An engineer or a switchman who could not clearly distinguish between red and white or green would be likely at any time to send a trainload of passengers to destruction. And the perils from colorblindness are largely increased by the fact that those afflicted with it are often not aware of it and count their eyesight as clear as anybody's.

Just as some colorblind people are not aware of their colorblindness, so it is spiritually. Those who are sinful are not always aware of their sinfulness, of their spiritual colorblindness. Of recent years the great railroad companies test the vision of their employees by the aid of skilled eye specialists, with the

32

result that from 10-25% of those who apply for positions as engineers and signal men are found to be deficient in color judgment. This is certainly a very pertinent illustration of the Scriptures we are studying. As the managers of railroads are heeding the cry of the newspapers and the public to beware of colorblindness, and are determined that the men who drive their trains shall know the difference between red and yellow, so the warning of Christ comes to every one of us, "Take heed therefore that the light which is in thee be not darkness" (Luke 11:35).

The Dangers of Self-Deception

There could be no more important warning than this. It is certainly a terrible thing to be self-deceived. Yet Jesus Himself says that some will come to Him in the day of judgment, and ask that the doors of heaven be opened to them, pleading in their own behalf that they have prophesied in the name of Christ, and in His name have cast out evil spirits, to whom the tenderhearted but righteous Christ will be compelled to say, "I never knew you: depart from me, ye that work iniquity" (Matt. 7:23). We want to be sure that our conscience is in harmony with the commandments of God's Word. If a colorblind engineer mistakes a red signal for a white one at an open drawbridge, the resulting calamity is as terrible to the railroad passengers as if he had deliberately defied a token of danger which he read correctly. If one violates the civil law unconsciously, he is not exempt from legal penalties because of his false sense of security. If a man has bought stolen goods without knowing it, their real owner can reclaim those goods at the holder's cost. If there is a flaw in the title of a man's homestead, he can be driven from that home mercilessly, no matter what he paid for it, no matter how much he is attached to it, no matter how necessary it is to the comfort or the safety of himself or his family. If his title is not sound, he must leave it. His colorblindness in reading the title does not make the false title a true one.

Isaiah declared that that which is true in the material world is also true in the spiritual world. How deep and impressive are his terrible words, "Woe unto them that call evil good, and good evil; that put darkness for light, and light for darkness; that put bitter for sweet, and sweet for bitter! Woe unto them that are wise in their own eyes, and prudent in their own sight!" (Isa. 5:20, 21). Watch out for spiritual colorblindness. You may cause great catastrophe to others and to yourself by having darkness in your heart and thinking that you have light.

THINK IT OVER

1. Have you ever thanked God for your eyesight?
2. As you read His Word, do you also thank Him for spiritual insights He gives you?
3. Why can we never accuse God of responsibility for evil? (See I John 1:5 and James 1:17.)
4. Are you willing to receive God's light with an open mind, or do you shut your eyes to certain portions of Scripture that you find it inconvenient to accept or practice?

4

What Your One Life Can Do
for Christ

All great work for Christ in the world has not been begun by committees, but by the consecration, self-sacrifice, and devotion of single individuals. And God wants you to realize what He can do through you as an individual. Never mind if you are not part of a great church, or of a great committee, you are an individual in whose heart the light of God is shining and out of whose heart the light of God can shine into the world. The greatest sermons do not always come from the pulpit, but from the lives of men and women like you and me, from our daily walk.

Displaying Christ in Our Daily Lives

"No man, when he hath lighted a candle," our Lord says, "putteth it in a secret place, neither under a bushel, but on a candlestick, that they which come in may see the light" (Luke 11:33). Our Christianity is not something to be put on for appropriate occasions and then carefully hidden away. It is our everyday life. The most influential pulpits are at our work-

35

benches, in our homes, and in our schoolrooms. Wherever we may be, whatever we may be doing, we are witnessing. We may not be able to win the lost by words, but we never know how many people we may win by example. We display the possessions of which we are proud. Is not Christ our greatest possession? Then why not display Him daily?

A young man, a skilled mechanic, was driving a visiting clergyman from his home town, fifty miles across the country, to another city. En route, they passed a huge factory consisting of perhaps twenty buildings scattered over several hundred acres. "Do you see that red brick building over there behind this gray stone one?" the mechanic asked. "I work on the second floor on the south side. There are 74 of us in that department and, so far as I know, I am the only one in all that crowd who ever goes to church or tries to live a Christian life. Sometimes I have to remind myself that, so far as that department is concerned, I am all there is of the Christian Church. If I do not do good work, then the Church has failed so far as those men are concerned. If I cannot be relied upon, then the Church is undependable. If I am careless, then some poor unfortunate devil may have to pay for the Church's carelessness. It is pretty serious business being the Church in the midst of 74 other people."

What One Life Can Accomplish When Dedicated to Soul-Winning

You and I are the Church among those who work with us. The young man was conscious of his responsibility for witnessing, but seems to have been lacking in aggressiveness. Was his faith weak? Did he think that, since he was the only Christian, his life might not be able to count for Christ? There is an inscription on a highway plaque in a small Minnesota town which reads, "On September 1, 1894, a forest fire swept over this area and 450 people lost their lives." As a person reads this sign, he cannot help asking himself, "What do you suppose started that fire?" Along the highways throughout our national forests we see signs urging tourists to be careful with fires. Each has a stern warning that a single match carelessly thrown away can start a conflagration. One match seems insignificant, but think of its tremendous potential. One Christian can be a radiant witness for his Master if he will only resolve to do so and dedicate his life to soul-winning.

> My life shall touch a dozen lives
>   Before this day is done;
> Leave countless marks for good or ill
>   Ere sets this evening's sun.
> Shall fair or foul its imprint prove
>   On those my life shall hail;
> Shall benison my impress be,
>   Or shall a blight prevail?
> From out each point of contact
>   Of my life with other lives,
> Flows ever that which helps the one
>   Who for the summit strives.
> The troubled souls encountered
>   Does it sweeten with its touch,
> Or does it more embitter those
>   Embittered over-much?
> Does love in every handclasp flow
>   In sympathy's caress?
> Do those that I have greeted know
>   A newborn hopefulness?
> Are tolerance and charity
>   The keynote of my song,

As I go plodding onward
With earth's eager, anxious throng?
— Author Unknown

An Example of a Dedicated Soul-Winner

Melvin Harper is manager of an eight-thousand-acre buckeye ranch and rice farm near Bay City, Texas. "Lord, send me cowboys who aren't Christians," is his daily prayer. Why? Because encouraging cowboys and youngsters to live for Christ is a kind of divine calling for the man who was the nation's top bronco buster and steer rider for more than ten years. Through the personal interest of a pastor who began visiting Harper at the ranch and said he wanted to learn to ride and handle cattle, the veteran rodeo performer started attending church regularly and made his decision for Christ. Soon he began teaching a class of boys, but he doubts that he was doing much witnessing for Christ.

A new pastor came to the church, and one day the rugged ranch manager went by to see him. Their conversation soon turned to religion. Melvin asked his new pastor, "Do you believe in the Lord?" After receiving a quick and affirmative answer, Melvin continued, "Then if me and you prayed to God, believed in Christ, and asked for something, would we get it?" The prayer that followed is one which Pastor Eaves will never forget. Melvin and his pastor prayed that God would let him become a soul-winner.

Melvin didn't sleep much that night, and at four o'clock in the morning he was fully dressed and on his way to the home of a lost friend. He arrived before daylight and prayed as he waited in a pick-up truck for the lights to come on in the house. The friend was won to Christ, and that was only the beginning. Melvin's pastor estimates that he has already won more than fifty people to the Lord. Five cowboys at the ranch have become Christians, and in his Sunday school class of thirteen-year-old boys, 24 have accepted Christ in one year.

When asked about the greatest thrill of his life, Melvin told about being the only rider one year to stay mounted on the nation's wildest and best bucking rodeo horse in Madison Square Garden and in Houston. "But," said Melvin, "this kind of thrill doesn't compare with winning a boy, his parents, and a cowhand to Christ."

Don't Hide Your Light — Let It Shine for Jesus

How many have you won? Are you the light that points men and women to Christ every day as they rub shoulders with you? Jesus says, "Ye are the light of the world" (Matt. 5:14). Don't hide it. Let it shine. The heart of God our Father yearns over the perishing souls of men. He hungers for the cooperation of men to reach the hearts of other men. And this is one of the greatest mysteries, that an omnipotent God who is able to save everybody without the interference of anybody, still desires your cooperation and mine in witnessing, in giving out His light.

At every stage of life, God approaches us saying, "Go work." During what remains of life's brief day, "Go work . . . in my vineyard" (Matt. 21:28). I need you to help in the salvation of a myriad of souls.

Whatever may be our chosen vocation in life, we should not stand idly by without witnessing for the Master. Even in the area of stewardship, the Master would say to us, "Go work in My vineyard. Administer your money, time, and influence for Me." Oh, that the urgency of God's compassion may touch and move us! To delay may mean to be too late.

A Witness That Came Too Late

Far up the Amazon River, a Baptist missionary was using

a flannelgraph to aid her in telling a group of schoolchildren about Jesus. As she talked, an elderly man with stooped shoulders and gray hair joined the children. He listened with rapt attention as the missionary told the story of God's grace as it is revealed in Christ. After the children were dismissed, the old man came up to the missionary with this question: "May I ask, Madam, if this interesting and intriguing story is true?"

"Of course," the missionary said; "it is in the Word of God."

With countenance and voice revealing his doubt, the old gentleman said, "This is the first time in my life that I have ever heard that one must give his life to Jesus to have forgiveness from sin and to have life with God forever." Then with a note of finality he concluded, "This story cannot be true or else someone would have come before now to tell it. I am an old man. My parents lived their lives and died without ever having heard this message. It cannot be true or someone would have come sooner." Although she tried hard, the missionary could not convince the old gentleman of this truth from God's Word. Turning to make his way back into the darkness of the jungle and the darkness of sin, he kept repeating the words, "It cannot be true; it cannot be true, or someone would have come sooner."

Three out of every four people living in the world never heard of this wonderful Savior, the light of the world. It is pathetic. Who is responsible? God has given us the privilege of being His co-workers. Are we failing Him? Is your light hidden under a bushel or does it shine?

What Would He Say?

If He should come today,
And find my hands so full
Of future plans, however fair,

40

In which my Savior has no share,
    What would He say?

If He should come today,
And find my love so cold,
My faith so very weak and dim,
I had not even looked for Him,
    What would He say?

If He should come today,
And find I had not told
One soul about my Heavenly Friend
Whose blessings all my way attend,
    What would He say?

If He should come today,
Would I be glad — quite glad?
Remembering He had died for all,
And none, through me, had heard His
call;
    What would He say?
                                — Grace E. Troy

THINK IT OVER

1. Do you have some earthly possession — a work of art, something you have made yourself, your family, for instance — of which you are rightfully proud? Do you display or speak about them often?
2. Do you have an even greater heavenly treasure —Jesus Christ, in whom you have found salvation? Do you display Him by your actions, and speak to others about Him?
3. Are you letting your light shine for Jesus, or hiding it under a bushel?

5

Using and Guarding the Light of the Soul

In this parable that the Lord has given us in Luke 11:33-36, Jesus Christ is the light and we are His candlestick. He is in us, and we are the means by which the world sees Him. As light, the Lord could not be hidden. It is our responsibility to set Him on the candlestick, not to put Him under a bushel basket. That's the whole parable. The light that is in you — is it in a secret place? Is it hidden?

"Oh," you may say, "this relationship between God and me is a very private matter. I just cannot take a trumpet and tell the whole world who Jesus is." But the Lord Jesus said that He is the light, and the light is not to be hidden under a bushel. The light is there to shine. Being His witnesses as individuals, we must not hide the light of God.

If you do not see Jesus, it is not because He has hidden Himself in darkness, but because your eyes are blinded. And if you do see Jesus and others around you do not, it is not because He is not a shining light, but because you have taken that light and put it in a secret place instead of letting it shine for all to see.

Light is not just for the rich, the wise, the strong, but for everybody. The teachings of the Lord Jesus are the common inheritance of those who labor and are heavy-laden. We must never discriminate in giving out the light of Christ, even as He does not discriminate in giving out His light to all people. The glorious Gospel light is for all who sit in darkness and long for the light of God. Share His light, and the more you and I share it, the more His light will shine in our own hearts.

Take Care That Your Light Does Not Grow Dim

It is clearly suggested in the text that, after having our minds and hearts illuminated by a conscience instructed by the Word of God and clarified by the Holy Spirit, something may come in to interfere with the light and turn it into darkness. "The light of the body is the eye: therefore when thine eye is single, thy whole body also is full of light; but when thine eye is evil, thy body also is full of darkness. Take heed therefore," our Master says, "that the light which is in thee be not darkness."

There is a danger that there may be dimming of the light that is within us. What is suggested here is certainly verified by history and observation. It is worth our while to note some of the things that bring about this sad eclipse of the soul. Anything that corrupts, or degrades, or debauches the soul; anything that mars its innocence, or robs it of its purity, will at the same time dull the keenness of its perception as to what is right and what is wrong. Innocence is often compared to cleanness or whiteness, while guilt is described by the words dark, black, mire, and dirt. Conscience is like a glass through which the light streams. But if we rub coal dust or smut of any sort over the glass, the light will shine through it but dimly. And if we cover the glass with a sufficient coat of filth, it will not shine through at all. So sin makes foul the glass of the soul. Where the light shines clearly and the man has no doubt at all about what is right, if he yields to temptation, and sinful thoughts make conquest of him, it will be as though tar stained the glass in his window. And if he continues to sin, and impure thoughts come to get possession of his soul, the light from heaven will finally be shut out entirely.

Examples of Those Whose Consciences Became Defiled and Darkened

The Philistines would never have been able to put out Samson's eyes had he not yielded to the sinful embrace of Delilah, who put out the inner eye of his conscience. When by his sins the inner light had been shut out, it was not long before he lost the outer also.

When God sent His angels to Sodom to lead Lot and his family out from under the doom that overhung that wicked city, and the mob gathered round the house determined to do violence to the strangers, the messengers of God smote the Sodomites with blindness. But their own lusts and wickedness had already changed the light of their souls into darkness, and that was the cause of the outer blindness which fell upon them.

Herod would never have stained his hands with the murder of John the Baptist had he not first debauched his conscience in his life of sin with the wicked Herodias. Having broken the seventh commandment, the sixth stood too near it to be safe for long.

We have illustrations on every hand. Who does not know of some man who had a clear head and good business abilities whose judgment in business, or in politics, or in any question relating to the practical affairs of life, was trustworthy and valuable; but as he gave himself over to some sin like that of drunkenness, and as the sin came to have mastery over him and he was debauched by it, he lost his clearness of mind, his keenness of wit, and his judgment, and he no longer was regarded as a safe counselor in any matter of importance.

How true to our modern experience are the words of Solomon: "Who hath woe? Who hath sorrow? Who hath contentions? Who hath babbling? Who hath wounds without cause? who hath redness of eyes? They that tarry long at the wine; they that go to seek mixed wine" (Prov. 23:29, 30). We do not wonder at the earnestness of the exhortation which follows, "Look not thou upon the wine when it is red, when it giveth his colour in the cup, when it moveth itself aright. At the last it biteth like a serpent, and stingeth like an adder. Thine eyes shall behold strange women, and thine heart shall utter perverse things. Yea, thou shalt be as he that lieth down in the midst of the sea, or as he that lieth upon the top of a mast. They have stricken me, shalt thou say, and I was not sick; they have beaten me, and I felt it not: when shall I awake? I shall seek it yet again" (Prov. 23:31-35). And why will he seek it again when he arises out of his drunken slumber? Why will he seek it, though his head aches, and his soul is full of loathing, and his wife's heart breaks, and his children hide their heads in shame? The answer is simple, he will seek it again because the sin that has corrupted and debauched his heart has at the same time darkened his mind and changed the inner light into darkness. How careful we must be to guard that inner light against being dimmed or altogether extinguished by sin.

THINK IT OVER

1. In this parable, who is the light and who is the candlestick?
2. How can the light within us be dimmed?

3. Give an illustration from Scripture where sin overcoming a man's spiritual light actually led to physical blindness.

6

How to Keep Your Light Shining Brightly

We have considered some of the sins that destroy the inner light and change the light of heaven within us into darkness. One of these against which we must guard is bribery. It is possible for the soul to be bribed so that a man cannot judge impartially and righteously.

In Deuteronomy we have the record of the qualifications that Moses required of a judge. One of these was that he should not "take a gift." The reason that he gives for this is that "a gift doth blind the eyes of the wise" (Deut. 16:19).

When Samuel was challenging his enemies to bring any accusation of evil against him he asked, "Of whose hand have I received any bribe to blind mine eyes therewith?" (I Sam. 12:3). Many a soul is bribed by the greed for money. The offer of riches is often the devil's bribe to get people to listen to him.

Money Is Not Evil in Itself

The Bible declares, "The love of money is the root of all evil" (I Tim. 6:10). It is not the money itself that is evil but the love of it. A man who is greedy of gain has double vision. He cannot distinguish clearly in questions of honesty. He is not an impartial judge when he sees an opportunity to get his hands on gold. To such a man material things assume an altogether false proportion and he is ready to exchange spiritual wealth of infinite value for treasures that are transitory and soon pass away.

The Parable of the Rich Farmer

Jesus sets this forth very clearly in the Parable of the Rich Farmer whose fields brought forth so plentifully that he said, "I will pull down my barns, and build greater; and there will I bestow all my fruits and my goods. And I will say to my soul, Soul, thou hast much goods laid up for many years; take thine ease, eat, drink, and be merry. But God said unto him, Thou fool, this night thy soul shall be required of thee: then whose shall those things be, which thou hast provided? So is he that layeth up treasure for himself, and is not rich toward God" (Luke 12:18-21). Few people escape this sort of temptation; the devil bribes the poor as well as the rich by the promise of material gain at the cost of spiritual poverty.

Jesus Our Example in Resisting Satan's Bribes

Jesus, who was tempted at all points like as we are, met this temptation squarely when in the wilderness the devil took Him to the mountaintop and showed Him "all the kingdoms of the world, and the glory of them; and saith unto him, All these things will I give thee, if thou wilt fall down and worship me" (Matt. 4:8, 9). But Christ, who was the light of the world, whose eye was single, whose whole body was full of light, exclaimed without hesitation, "Get thee hence, Satan: for it is written, Thou shalt worship the Lord thy God, and him only shalt thou serve" (Matt. 4:10). The devil left Him then, and he will flee from us if we resist him with the same single-eyed devotion.

The Danger of Greed for Applause or Power

Sometimes the soul is bribed, and the light within us is changed into darkness, through greed of applause or power. This is coming at us from the top instead of from the bottom, as was the case with money. Greed of gain darkens our light by taking us down into the cellar of our natures and making us grovel in the earth and dig like moles for yellow dirt. Greed for applause and power takes us to the pinnacle of the temple and destroys our light and unbalances our judgment of what is right by making us dizzy and confused. "Pride goeth before destruction," we are told (Prov. 16:18). It is true, because the proud man becomes giddy at his own eminence and is no longer true in his moral vision.

Solomon says again, "Seest thou a man wise in his own conceit? There is more hope of a fool than of him" (Prov. 26:12). That is evidently true. For if a man has but little wisdom, and is conscious of it, he may ask wisdom of God, who "giveth to all men liberally, and upbraideth not" (James 1:5). Such a man in his weakness, being led by the divine light, may walk in safety, for the light from heaven makes the way so plain that if a man's heart is right, though he be a wayfaring man and a fool, he need not err in the path (see Isa. 35:8). But if a man is wise in his own conceits, then he will be indifferent to the light from heaven. He will shut his eyes to the warnings of Scripture. The light that is within him will be changed into darkness and great will be that darkness.

How to Escape Darkness and Walk in the Light

But thank God we are not left in darkness as to how we may keep the light that is within us, and make sure that our whole body shall be full of light. The Lord Jesus said, "Walk while ye have the light, lest darkness come upon you....While ye have light, believe in the light, that ye may be the children of light" (John 12:35, 36). And John, who got so near to the heart of Christ, says, "This then is the message which we have heard of him, and declare unto you, that God is light, and in him is no darkness at all. If we say that we have fellowship with him, and walk in darkness, we lie, and do not the truth. But if we walk in the light, as he is in the light, we have fellowship one with another, and the blood of Jesus Christ his Son cleanseth us from all sin" (I John 1:5-7).

This surely suggests to us very clearly how we may keep the light of heaven shining brightly in our hearts and minds. We are to walk in the light. We are not to sit down in it and expect that, without any exertion on our part, the light of joy and peace and truth will always illuminate our souls. We are to *walk* in the light. That takes effort. We are to seek day by day to live according to the commandments of God; and in living an obedient life we shall have light. The Psalmist said, "The entrance of thy words giveth light" (Ps. 119:130). And in Proverbs 6:23 we read, "The commandment is a lamp; and the law is light." We must walk in the light of God's countenance. "Blessed are the people that know the joyful sound: they shall walk, O Lord, in the light of thy countenance" (Ps. 89:15).

Walk in the Light of the Holy Spirit and in Fellowship with Christ

And especially are we to walk in the light of the Holy Spirit. It is essential to have the illumination of the Holy Spirit constantly infilling us. This infilling is not a once-and-for-all affair, it is a constant and repeated infilling. It is like putting oil into a lamp, so to speak, so that it may keep on shining. "The

Spirit itself beareth witness with our spirit, that we are the children of God" (Rom. 8:16), the children of light.

We are to walk in the fellowship of Jesus Christ, who says, "He that followeth me shall not walk in darkness, but shall have the light of life" (John 8:12). God help us to live worthy of our great inheritance.

The Apostle Paul says, "Ye are all the children of light, and the children of the day: we are not of the night, nor of darkness" (I Thess. 5:5). "For ye were sometimes darkness, but now are ye light in the Lord: walk as children of light" (Eph. 5:8).

How to Come Out of Spiritual Darkness into Fullness of Light

But someone says, "I'm a poor sinner. It is all dark to me. I have sinned against God and against my conscience. I have sinned against my mother's prayers. I have sinned against the knowledge of the words of Christ. I'm in the darkness and I do not see the way out."

Thank God, His Word can show you the way through the Lord Jesus, who says, for the benefit of one in just your condition, "I am come a light into the world, that whosoever believeth on me should not abide in darkness" (John 12:46). That "whosoever" includes you. In whatever spot of darkness you may dwell, Jesus becomes the light of the world for you, to shed in your heart the glory of God that shines in His face. Turn your face toward that light in humble faith, and you too will become "the light of the world," as He calls His disciples in Matthew 5:14. You may not think your little light can have much influence in dispelling the darkness of the world, but added to millions of other little lights it can help to reach to the farthest corners of earth.

An Australian bush preacher went to a little church in the

53

bush to preach. It was dusk when he arrived and the place was without light, and he wondered what to do about it. Presently he saw twinkling lights moving about through the bush. His congregation was arriving. Each person carried a hurricane lamp, and as they came in they placed their lamps upon a shelf around the chapel wall, and soon the whole place was flooded with light. Each had contributed light that had dispelled the darkness. Your share is needed in a world that desperately needs the illumination of the Gospel.

THINK IT OVER

1. Supply the first three words to make the following quotation read correctly: "___ ___ ___ money is the root of all evil."
2. Name two ways in which it is evil to acquire money.
3. What is dangerous to the soul in seeking applause and power? How can our coming out of darkness into light help to dispel the darkness of this world?

7

The Single Eye and
the Evil Eye Contrasted

Our Master said, "The light of the body is the eye." In some versions the word "light" is rendered "lamp." The comparison, at first examination, may seem inappropriate, for a lamp is an object that distributes light, and the eye an organ that receives it. How can it be, then, that the lamp of the body is the eye? Put a lamp into a darkened room and the room is lightened by its radiance, but put an eye into that room and the darkness still remains. Why, therefore, in this parable that our Lord has given us, should an eye be compared to a lamp? Because, like a lighted lamp, the physical eye furnishes the light for the entire body. True, it's not its own light, but it takes the light that comes from outside and furnishes it for the entire personality of man.

I would have you note when our Lord says, "The lamp of the body is the eye," the words "Is the lamp of the body" is the predicate. It tells us what the eye is. And it is put forward here for emphasis. Actually, the wording should be, "The eye is the lamp of the body." The lamp, that is, the eye, is the subject, and the lamp of the body is the predicate. It doesn't say the eye is *a* lamp of the body, but it's *the* lamp of the body. Now the article "the" used with the predicate shows that the predicate is identical with the subject. In other words, the eye of yours is the lamp of your body. The eye and the lamp are one. Without the lamp there could be no seeing in a dark room. Without your eye there could be no seeing that would enter and illuminate your personality.

Take the statement in I John 4:16, for instance, "God is love." Now there the word "love" is the predicate, but it is not preceded by the definite article "the." In Greek, it is "The God is love," not "The God is *the* love." Now, you can never reverse this and make the predicate the subject. You can never say that "love is God," because then this inanimate characteristic of love becomes Deity. It is absolutely wrong to say "love is God." "The God is love." Love is not identical with God. He is not an abstract quality; He is a personality.

Therefore, when our Lord says here in Luke 11:34, "The lamp of the body is the eye," there is a definite article before the word "lamp" and there is a definite article before the word "eye." And what this means is that the eye is identical to the lamp. The eye is the only means by which light comes into our whole personality and the lamp, an outside light, is the only way by which light is given to us.

The Eye — the Heart of Man — Determines How We See People, God, and Life

And, of course, what our Lord meant is that the eye is the heart of man, and on the condition of the heart depends what we see: how we see other people, how we see God, how we see the situations of life. We may see them as they are or we may pervert them. What our Savior wanted to teach by the analogy of the eye and the lamp is that everything we see depends on the condition of the lamp. If the lamp is dim, we won't see very clearly. If our eye is dim, diseased, the whole body will be darkened. Similarly, if the lamp is burning brightly, we see things as they are. We recognize the books upon the table and the photographs upon the wall. But if the lamp is flickering or smoky, everything is distorted or obscured; and so, says the Lord, it is with the eye. If we are colorblind, we cannot see the glorious redness of the rose. If we are shortsighted we cannot see the friend who is signaling to us from a little distance. If we suffer from impending cataracts, a friend may sit on the next chair to us, yet all that we distinguish is a shadow. Still, the rose is red, though we cannot see it in our colorblindness. Still, the friend is waving to us or seated by our side. There is nothing the matter with reality. The trouble is that we are seeing badly.

Now the Lord tells us that the eye can be either single (healthy), or it can be evil. And this means the heart of man, because as the eye is the element by which the body is lightened, so the heart of man is that organ by which the spiritual self is enlightened. The heart can be single or evil. "When thine eye is single," that's one condition. We'll see what "single" means later. Or "when thine eye is evil," that's the other condition. The Greek word for "evil" here is *poneeros*. There are two opposite adjectives here indicating moral conditions, "single" and "evil."

What the Lord Jesus Wanted People to See

I would have you note, however, what the object is that the Lord wanted the people to see. For the object has been strongly presented in the previous context. You remember that the people were asking Jesus for a further sign than the healing of a deaf, dumb, and blind man. "Give us signs so that we may believe," was their cry. And the Lord said that no sign would be given them except the sign of Jonah, who was three days and three nights in the belly of the fish. Even so the Son of man would be three days and three nights in the earth and He would rise again. "He is your sign," Jesus was telling them, "and you don't recognize it."

And then you remember He spoke of the Queen of Sheba who came a thousand miles to hear Solomon's wisdom. And of the Ninevites who believed when finally Jonah preached to them. And our Lord says in effect, "There is someone here that is greater than Solomon and Jonah, and you don't recognize Him, you don't see Him. You have eyes but you don't see the reality of the person who is among you."

Why do these scribes and Pharisees fail to see what is before their very eyes? It is because their organ of spiritual sight, the heart, is not single but wicked. Remember, the word "wicked" here referred to the eye, and is the same word that our Lord used to describe the generation in which He lived. "You, an evil generation, *poneera.*"

What the Evil Eye Cannot See

And now He calls the eye evil. First of all, let us examine the word "single." In Greek it is *haplous,* which actually means "without fold." When we fold something we may hide something in that fold. So the eye should be without fold, without duplicity, without ulterior motive, hidden back in some fold. In other words, the Lord is telling these Pharisees that were objecting to His being the final sign of God, "There is a fold in your thinking. You are hiding something. Your thinking, your heart, is not single. Not everything is seen properly that must be seen in Me. You do not see me as greater than Solomon; you do not see me as greater than Jonas; and the reason is, not that I don't have greater qualities than both Solomon and Jonas, but that in your heart, in your eye, you are evil. And being evil, you cannot see the good that is in Me."

And isn't that true of human nature? If we look at somebody and we don't like him, we fail to see the good in him. If our inner eye is evil, how can we see what is good in others? Well, the word "evil" here, *poneeros*, "thine eye is evil," means actively wicked. There are two Greek words for "evil" — *kakos*, which means evil in its constitution, in itself, but not necessarily trying to propagate evil. *Poneeros* means not only evil in its constitution, but also describes one who tries to propagate evil, who is actively wicked. And this is why one of the names of the devil is *poneeros*, "the wicked one." He is not only wicked in himself but he tries to propagate evil everywhere to everyone. He is hostile toward God and he expresses it in his daily activities.

This generation, our Lord says, is evil, not merely bad, but endeavoring to propagate that evil. And the eye can be evil, actively wicked. That means it looks at something with a view to capitalizing on its evil possibilities. For instance, the wicked eye will look at a beautiful woman and say, "Why should she be somebody else's and not mine?" And it leads to its possessor going ahead to find ways and means by which he can appropriate that woman who doesn't belong to him.

When an evil heart looks at Jesus it sees only what these Pharisees and scribes saw, a man who was in league with Beelzebub, the devil, a man who had insufficient signs as credentials, a man who was a glutton and winebibber. You can look at a person who eats a hearty meal, and you can say one of two things about him: "He eats to sustain himself," or "Oh, look at him eat! I've never seen anybody devour as much food as he does," while in fact, you may have appetites even more gross. It all depends on your disposition, on your attitude.

Contrast between What the "Single Eye" and the "Evil Eye" See in the Same Objects or Circumstances

Our ability to see clearly depends on the eye, the disposition of the heart, the Lord Jesus Christ says. If a person's eye is single, then only can he discover reality, the truth about life as he experiences it. For instance, if sickness comes your way, how do you look at it? It all depends on how your inner eye, your heart, is disposed toward God. You may see it as a punishment from God and say, "Look at what God is doing to me!" Or you can see it as an expression of the goodness of God. If your inner vision is evil, you will see God as evil in permitting suffering in your life; but if your heart is single, you say, "God cannot be a source of sweet and bitter toward me; He's my Father; I'm His child; He can only be the source of good toward me. And whether I experience sickness or health, abundance or privation, He is still my Father, treating me kindly for my ultimate good." But if your eye is wicked, you will say, "How cruel God is! Look at what He is doing to me!"

I remember when I had an almost fatal car accident recently and was taken to the hospital. In the middle of the night, while I was in agony, they brought in a young man. It was dark, and I couldn't see him. He began to curse God volubly. And from the hospital's public address system, there came the question, "What religion are you, Protestant or Catholic?" This young man shouted, "Heathen! I don't believe in God. Look, if God existed, if God was there, He never would have permitted me to have what I have."

You know, if a person says this, his eye, his heart, is evil. In the midst of my agony, I couldn't take that. I lifted up my voice, although I couldn't see the young man in my room, and said, "Young man, remember that there will be a day of judgment. Don't hate Jesus. You don't see what He is to you

60

because your eyes are blinded."

If we do not see in the Lord Jesus Christ a greater than Solomon, a greater than Jonah, it's not because He's not, it's because our eye is not single, it's evil. Oh, for the cleansing of our hearts! Love sees people as they really are. Hatred sees them as it desires them to appear. To appreciate all that there is in music, you must first love it. To appreciate the good in somebody, you must first love him. To appreciate God as He really is, you must first love Him.

A girl who received a book from a young man read it and said, "What a tiresome book!" The young man said, "Did you notice who wrote it?" And she looked at the front page and saw that her lover was the author. She began to read it again, and at the end she said, "I never read a greater book." What made the difference? Her relationship to the writer.

Look at God. Is He good or evil? It all depends on whether you are single in heart or evil in heart. If you look at Jesus, you may see Him either as a deceiver or as a Savior. What makes the difference? Your attitude, your eye.

Two people may look at an object. One of them, having a healthy eye, may see the thing in its reality. Another, having defective eyesight, may see it as distorted, different from what it is. Have you not been looked at differently by different people? I'm sure that not all the people who know you think the same of you. Some may think you are an awful person. Others may believe that you are good. What makes the difference? It depends on their attitude and their relationship to you.

Why People Vary in Their Views about the Lord Jesus

And so it is with the Lord Jesus Christ. We look at Him and we decide on Him variably. In Matthew 13:13-16 our Lord recognized this tendency and addressed Himself to it: "Therefore speak I to them in parables," He said, "because they seeing see not; and hearing they hear not, neither do they understand. And in them is fulfilled the prophecy of Esaias [Isaiah], which saith, By hearing ye shall hear, and shall not understand; and seeing ye shall see, and shall not perceive: for this people's heart is waxed gross, and their ears are dull of hearing, and their eyes they have closed; lest at any time they should see with their eyes, and hear with their ears, and should understand with their heart, and should be converted, and I should heal them. [Healing here is spiritual healing. Not every time that the word heal is used in the New Testament does it refer to physical healing.] But blessed are your eyes, for they see: and your ears, for they hear."

We have an illustration of how people see, depending on the condition of their eyes, in Mark 8:22-26. The Lord healed a blind man of Bethsaida. He then asked him whether he could see anything. His reply was that he saw "men as trees, walking." These men were not trees, of course; though they appeared so to him. He wasn't seeing rightly. The lamp was flickering and objects were distorted. Similarly, what we see spiritually depends on what we are spiritually. As the lamp conditions the aspects of the room, so does the inward eye condition everything. Our life and character condition what we see.

Let us take Christ as an example. He moved in the midst of His contemporaries, shining in the splendor of good deeds. He was set on a candlestick, as it were — visible, conspicuous, radiant in loveliness of life. Yet some said that He was beside Himself, and some that He was a glutton and winebibber, and others that He cast out devils by Beelzebub. They saw Him by the dim light of what they were. They saw in Him the carpenter but not the Lord.

How We See Jesus Depends on What We Are in the Inner Light of Our Souls

What we discern the Lord to be demonstrates the life that we have been living. What we think of Jesus speaks of what we are. And what we see in others ultimately depends on what we are also. When the inward lamp is bright, we see reality. When it is smoky, everything is smutty. The judgments that we pass on other people (and we pass such judgments daily) are always judgments of ourselves. When our Lord said, "Judge not, that ye be not judged" (Matt. 7:1), He was not thinking of an external judgment; He meant that what we see in other people reveals our real character, and on that is based the judgment of eternity.

"The lamp of the body is the eye." Jesus speaks of the effect that the way a person sees himself has on others. The person with the single eye has his whole body full of light. *Photeinos* is the Greek word: "shining, full of light." The man with the wicked eye has his whole body full of darkness.

The eye does not see for its own sake; it sees for the entire body. All the bodily members, mouth, hands, feet, and so on, will act as the eye, (the heart of man) sees and directs. The eye that sees in Jesus more than Solomon and Jonah will draw the whole body into the light, to follow, trust, worship, and obey Jesus. The eye that sees Him as a friend of Satan will put his whole body into darkness: the mouth to oppose Him with words, the feet to dog Him, the hands at last to drag Him to the cross. That is darkness indeed. If the lamp be dimmed, everything is dull. If the inward eye has a cataract, loveliness itself is but a blur. That is why certain people could look at Jesus who was the altogether lovely One, and only see a glutton and a winebibber.

The Way Jesus Saw People and Objects Reveals Who He Is

It is there that our Lord reveals the glory of His nature. Judge the Lord Jesus by what He saw, and you touch the essence of the Son of God. He saw the Kingdom in a mustard seed, and the adoring and repentant woman in the harlot. He saw the solid rock in Simon, and the lover in the Son of Thunder. He saw in a child the citizen of heaven, in a bit of bread His broken body, in a cup of common wine His sacred blood. The more we become like Jesus the more of His glory we can see.

And the man without an eye might as well be without the sun, so far as light is concerned. The eye is as needful as a lamp if a man is to see. The brightest light is of no use to the person who has no eye. Therefore the saying, "The light of the body is the eye," is true. Christ shines in vain if His light cannot enter our souls.

How to Have the Full Light of Jesus in Your Heart

It is the Holy Spirit who makes us truly willing to know the truth and clears our mental eye. Most men, in their natural state, have no will to see the light of God. Their foolish hearts are darkened. A man will not see those truths against which he is naturally at enmity. If a man wills to see the truth and submit himself to the enlightenment of the Holy Spirit, he will not be left in darkness. When a man does not want to see, he cannot see. When he is determined not to learn, when truth is unpalatable to him, when he designedly twists it from its meaning, then his eye is diseased and the light is hindered from its due effect. The only way this light of Jesus Christ can come into his heart, is his permitting the Holy Spirit to bring it in and to let it change him and make him a new creature.

Holy Ghost, with light divine,
  Shine upon this heart of mine;
Chase the shade of night away
  Turn my darkness into day.
— Andrew Reed

THINK IT OVER

1. In what way can a lamp be compared to the human eye?
2. What was it that the Lord Jesus wanted the "sign-seekers" of His generation to see?
3. Explain in your own words what Jesus meant by the words, "When thine eye is *single.*" What did He mean by the word "single"?
4. Is your eye "single" or "evil" in its assessments of the trials and troubles that come your way?
5. How can your inner darkness be turned to light?

8

Certain Things That Can Darken the Eye of the Soul

In Luke 11:35 our Lord tells us that there are certain things that can darken the eye of the soul. He says, "Take heed therefore that the light which is in thee [that is to say, Jesus Christ being the light of the world] be not darkness." It is possible for the light of the Gospel to become darkness in us. Now, what are the causes of this partial illumination? Why do many Christians fail to see the whole truth? Jesus is intimating that they may lapse into deplorable errors, that they may overlook directions and duties as clear to others as the noonday.

For instance take two Christians arguing about giving. One says, "Well, I don't see where the New Testament teaches that we ought to tithe our income." And he gives a dime, or a dollar to God's work, and thinks he has done his duty. He is only partially illumined. Is the reason found in some necessary limitation of his moral sense? Men's intellectual powers are always partial and imperfect. There is no such thing as absolute genius, the beholding with open vision the

67

universality of things. And it may be thought that there is a necessary corresponding qualification of the faculty of the individual conscience.

Let me give you an example: A sculptor who appreciates form is sometimes constitutionally incapable of appreciating color; and it may be inferred that we are liable to suffer from a similar qualification of the moral sense. Now, it is indeed impossible for any finite creature to comprehend or see all around the infinite truths of righteousness, but it is possible for all to apprehend the whole truth, to sympathize with it in its catholicity, its fullness, its proportion, its manifold beauty and splendor. No man as a philosopher may comprehend the whole truth of things. But every man may discern the moral law in all its versatility and wide-reaching delicate applications.

Christ tells us in this text that the eye is the lamp of the body, and so long as the eye is undiseased and uninjured we walk in light; but if the eye be impaired, we walk in darkness and insecurity, according to the degree of its imperfection. So we have an inner organ of perception and illumination. Everything depends upon the integrity of this organ, because if it is sound and pure we walk in the light. But if it is injured, dark places appear in our mind, in our character, in our life.

The question, of course, arises, How may we injure the eyes of our moral understanding? What are the things that darken the eye of the soul, our heart and conscience? We must define them so that we may guard against them.

Prejudice Can Darken Our Inner Light

The first one is prejudice. A man conceives that he has light already, by virtue of inheritance. He thinks that because his ancestors had it, he also has it. He may have a family lamp, but the lamp may not give any light. He will not investigate when the light of God comes to him. He at once rejects it. The very supposition that he may be wrong he regards as an insult.

Are you prejudiced? Do you look at someone whom you do not like, and seeing that he is different in his life, that he walks with Jesus, do you say, "Can that man be a real Christian with no previous religious background? Look at my ancestry. I have been raised in this religion; and does he presume to be on a par with me?" You can become so prejudiced that you cannot see truth. Beware of prejudice. It can be a spot of darkness in your heart.

Laziness a Source of Darkness

Then there is another source of darkness, *laziness*. Some people are like those who sit in a dark room simply because they do not take the time and trouble to open the shutters and draw up the blinds. They are in darkness because they are lazy. They do not work. They do not do something about the darkness that exists around them. They are like Pilate who asked, "What is truth?" but never waited for an answer. They do not search the Scriptures or pray or take time to hear the Gospel and be enlightened. They are spiritually lazy. They do not work out their own salvation. Salvation indeed comes from God, without any merit of our own, by faith, plus nothing. But that salvation, that light of Jesus Christ within us, in order to continue to be absolute light, requires us to work out our salvation in daily life, and not just lazily accept it as a free ticket to heaven.

Gross Errors Darken the Heart

There is a third thing that may darken our hearts, and that is *gross error*. Errors come to us nowadays as respectable forms of thought, as certain religious practices. Is there a spiritual error, a Scriptural error, a theological error that darkens your soul? You may hold certain doctrines to be so precious that you can't see truth as a whole; you can't see the forest for the trees. They blind you, just like putting a fifty-cent piece over your eye so that you shut out the sun. You put a minor doctrine in the forefront of your thinking and the whole thrill and beauty and largeness of the Gospel is lost.

Do you harp on a particular doctrine, leaving all the other wonderful doctrines of the Gospel untouched? That means that there is a dark spot in your conscience. Those doctrines and fashions which were once considered heresies are accepted today and they are given the place of prominence. Beware of one doctrine becoming the whole of God's Word in your thinking.

Jealousy Perverts the Light of the Soul

Another thing that darkens the light that is in us is *jealousy.* Jealousy is a destructive presence which perverts the light of the soul. We have a prime example of this perversion in the Old Testament. When David was returning from his encounter with Goliath, a body of women who had gone out from the city to meet him accompanied his return with songs of triumph, and this was their song: "Saul hath slain his thousands, and David his ten thousands" (I Sam. 18:7). Saul heard the song and marked the contrast, and his soul was inflamed with the unclean fires of jealousy. "And Saul eyed David from that day and forward" (v. 9). His jealous eye was an untrue one and never saw David truly. It transformed the innocent into a monster and filled his vision with an entirely false and crooked world. Jealousy is perhaps the most malignant and tormenting of all human passions. When inflamed it is simply a mood of lunacy.

Mrs. Wesley was furiously jealous of her husband. His work set him in the relation of friend and counselor to many women. Among his helpers, too, and in the institutions that were springing up under his care, women were employed, and each one was for his half-insane wife an object of deadly suspicion.

Wesley on his part was apt to be tolerant in a masculine, large-minded way, of facts and relation to such women, which other women, even the best, would hardly forgive. Sally Ryan for example, the housekeeper at one of his orphanages, was a woman with a past. She was at this time only 33, but she had three husbands living and was separated from them all. Wesley was in constant correspondence with her, a fact which kindled his wife to fury.

She stole Wesley's correspondence to satisfy her doubts. She would travel 100 miles to see who were his companions at a particular stage of his preaching tour. Her fury threw her sometimes into paroxysms of mad violence and sometimes into acts of almost incredible treachery. She not only stole her husband's letters; she tampered with them so as to give them an evil sense and put them into the hands of his enemies to be published.

Beware of jealousy. It can make the light of God in your heart so dark you see only evil, never good, in anyone.

The Love of Sin and Pleasure Causes Spiritual Blindness

Another thing that can darken the eye of the soul is *the love of sin and pleasure.* Hedonism, the love of pleasure, is a cause of spiritual blindness. You remember Herod. It would seem that he saw some great truths and felt the power of them, but when John the Baptist said to him, concerning Herodias (his brother's wife), "It is not lawful for thee to have her" (Matt. 14:4), the king could not see his own sin.

Dazzled by forbidden things, we fail also to see the beauty of that righteousness which comes between us and the objects of our illicit desire. If you love sin, you cannot love the Savior. And if you love the Savior you must hate sin. Sin is the cataract that darkens the mental eye. Men cannot see truth because they love falsehood. The Gospel is not seen because it is too pure for their loose lives and lewd thoughts. Christ's holy example is too severe for the worldly-minded.

When you find that the rules in the Word of God are too strict to suit you, and you revolt against them, do you know why? It is because in your heart there is a love of sin. You will reject the Word of God and what it prescribes for a holy life, if deep in your heart there is the constant desire to have the pleasures of the flesh and the temporal benefits of sin. The Lord's Spirit is too pure for lovers of carnal pleasure. When people reject the doctrines of the Gospel they also tolerate laxity of morals and give predominance to the customs of the world.

You know, the Christian life is one of great freedom of choice. That is why in Christianity today we find all kinds of people. There are those who love the Lord and don't care about the pleasures of the world. On the other hand, there are those who love the pleasures of the world, and want only as much of the Gospel of the Lord Jesus as will assure heaven for them. That's the kind of Christianity that we are being conditioned to in the 20th century. How can men see, when sin has pricked their spiritual eyeballs?

Greed Can Pervert Our Vision of Christ

There is another thing that dims our spiritual eyes and deprives us of the ability to see clearly all that there is in Jesus Christ. *Greed* can pervert your vision of Christ. It can destroy the lamp of the soul. You can see quite clearly how it maimed the vision of Judas and destroyed the fairness of his judgments. You remember Judas' reaction when a woman came to express her devotion to the Lord by breaking an alabaster box of precious ointment to anoint his feet? Judas looked upon such a beautiful deed of devotion and sacrifice as a waste, instead of looking at it as it was, an expression of love from a passionately grateful heart (John 12:1-8).

Sometimes when people see others working day and night for the Lord, they ask "What kind of life is that? Doesn't he have some time for pleasure? Doesn't he want to make money?" Greed is not in the heart of those who want to please the Lord. He is all to them. Judas saw waste in an act of great love. He had lost the power to see the beauty of sacrifice.

And today many people ridicule those who sacrifice. They can't see it in a world like ours. They want to give the Lord as little as possible and receive from the world as much as possible. The love of money has changed the face of the spiritual world. Many Christians are ready to serve the Lord if they get paid enough, but not otherwise. Oh, how we need the spirit of sacrifice instead of the spirit of greed! In the long run, thirty pieces of silver were more alluring than his Lord to Judas Iscariot. May God help us. What is there that is procurable by this money which we desire, over and above the necessities of life? Is it anything of worth, anything lasting? Why then do we desire it so inordinately? Very often it obtains for us hell itself, fire everlasting, and torments without end. Remember how Judas threw that money away. It meant his destruction.

The glitter of gold is very injurious to the eye. The love of money is a cause of blindness, creating strange refractions, distortions, and eclipses. The rich young ruler said to Jesus, "All these things [commandments] have I kept from my youth up: what lack I yet? Jesus said unto him, If thou wilt be perfect, go and sell that thou hast, and give to the poor, and thou shalt have treasure in heaven: and come and follow me" (Matt. 19:20,21).

Which would you rather not lose, Jesus or your possessions? The young man saw much that he was going to have to let go, and so he preferred to keep his material goods rather than to take Jesus. Of all the dust thrown in men's eyes, none is more blinding than gold dust. The revenue of the opium traffic makes it impossible to realize the monstrousness of the destroying trade.

Now, if you have the opportunity of getting a job that requires moral compromises but pays more money, are you going to take that, or take a job that does not require compromises but pays less money?

These are the things that measure your spiritual eyesight and your devotion to Jesus Christ. In private life, covetousness works the same result, drawing a veil over the heart. Be very, very careful about avarice. How can a man value heaven when a present fortune is heaven enough for him? Mammon repays its worshipers with blinded eyes. What's the use of having your hands full of money and your eyes blinded to the beauty of Jesus Christ and to the riches of the Word of God? Which do you love more, the truth of the Word of God or riches, gold?

Pride Hides the Complete Glory of Christ from Our Eyes

Then there is that dangerous enemy of the soul, *pride*. A proud person can never see the complete glory of Jesus Christ. Do you know why? Because he is so taken up with his own importance. Watch pride. It is impossible to see the fullness of the truth if we allow the warpings and discolorations of vanity, self-sufficiency, and prejudice to take place in our hearts. Pride easily blinds us to the truths which most deeply and immediately concern us.

For instance, we need to beware of ecclesiastical bigotry. What about church pride? Yes, you should be proud of your church, of course, but you should be prouder of Christ. If you are too proud of your church, you will look down on people who belong to other churches, and fail to recognize that they too love the Lord Jesus Christ very dearly.

Be careful of loving and being proud of anybody more than of the One who gave His life for you. Your husband, your wife, your children, your parents might be willing to give their lives for you, but their sacrifice could only save you temporarily, not eternally. Jesus gave His life for you that He might save you from eternal death, and therefore you must love Him more than anyone else.

We need to beware of ecclesiastical bigotry, of theological prejudice. Are you majoring in some minor doctrine which excludes you from fellowship with other Christians beloved of God? That's pride. Beware of intellectual prepossessions and conceit. Nothing dims spiritual vision more than pride. Humility, teachableness, susceptibility of soul, we must earnestly covet and pursue these virtues. The nobler souls are teachable, ever open to the light. "That which I see not teach thou me" (Job 34:32). "Teach me thy way, O Lord" (Ps. 27:11). "Teach me thy statutes" (Ps. 119:12).

Beware of the person who always knows God's will absolutely, and is forever telling somebody else that what he is doing cannot be God's will. The know-it-all really knows very little, because his eyesight is dimmed by pride and he cannot see beyond his own nose. Let our prayer ever be, "Teach me, Lord, to do Thy will."

Who are the suppliants for the clearer light? Are they babes, simpletons, novices, ignoramuses — illiterate, inexperienced souls with the least vision and enlightenment? Surely

75

not. They are the seers, the poets, the princes of the intellectual world, the masters of those who know. It is precisely such royal souls as Moses, Job, Isaiah, David, Solomon, John, and Paul who are most conscious of imperfect knowledge and who seek most passionately for the fuller, all-illuminating light. If we live thus in simplicity of desire, in meekness of spirit, in all lowliness and openness of mind, praying that we may be filled with the riches of understanding, our whole body will be full of light. Beware of pride. Don't think yourself higher than your brothers and sisters. Don't think your denomination the best in the world. Think of others. They too love the Savior.

Egotism Dims Our Spiritual Insight

Another thing that dims spiritual eyesight is *egotism*. That's an insidious enemy of the soul. If can destroy the lens of moral judgment. The Pharisee who in his prayer could say,"I thank thee, that I am not as other men are" (Luke 18:11), had lost his capacity to truly see the publican. Self can be so obtrusive that the real brother is altogether hidden. A man who greatly admires himself can never adore God. He that is taken up with the conceit of his own righteousness will never see the righteousness of Christ. If he thinks himself pure he will never ask for that blood that cleanses from all sin. No man cries for grace till he perceives his own need of it. If we think ourselves rich, we shall never seek the riches of Christ. A man's own shadow is very often the means of keeping him in the dark.

Popularity, the Love of Praise, Causes Spiritual Blindness

Popularity, the love of praise, is a cause of spiritual blindness. The Pharisees saw many truths distinctly, but when He came who was the truth they saw no beauty that they should desire Him. And Christ gives the reason for their tragic oversight. "How can ye believe," He said, "which receive honour one of another, and seek not the honour which cometh from God only?" (John 5:44).

If all that you care for is the honor of men, you will not seek to honor Christ. The love of worldly honor prevented the Pharisees from believing on the lowly Messiah. To have a clear eye one must have a clean heart. The Beatitudes declare that the pure in heart shall see God, and hence the pure in heart see God's truth so as to appropriate it and delight in it.

We do not see the truths which cross our inclination. "If the eye can see whate'er it will, it cannot see whate'er it does not will." The grand condition of seeing clearly throughout the whole circle of thought and responsibility is to have a supreme regard to the will of God, having no disturbing personal delights, ambitions, or aims.

Sincerity, love of the sunlight, is the first condition of clear vision. The single eye sees clearly and sees all. Popularity, wanting others to think well of us, and not caring so much of what God thinks of us, is a desire of which we must be very careful. Are the opinions of others more important than the opinion of God about you? Popularity is one form of self-seeking. Do you seek it actively? Do you sacrifice principles so that you may be popular? Or are you able to withstand the criticism of others by taking a stand for Christ?

Ambition Can Become a God That Makes You Forget the True God

Of course, there are other forms of self-seeking which blind the spiritual eyesight. One of them is *ambition*, desire of honor and respect. When a person has set in front of his eyes

77

a certain worldly goal, whether it be success in business, or amassing wealth, or recognition in the professions, and that becomes his god, it is a very dangerous thing. You forget the real God and you cannot see what the Lord may have in store for you. It's good to be ambitious, but be careful that it does not steal from you your spiritual eyesight.

We must also watch out lest we blind our eyes from seeing how wonderful Jesus is, in the desire of honor from others, the desire to be highly respected.

If you find yourself going around with a chip on your shoulder because you think you are not receiving all the honor and respect due you, be very careful. Do not seek honor, do not seek respect, be content with that which God allows you to have. If you see self all the time, you are on dangerous ground.

One day a wealthy old miser visited a rabbi, who took him by the hand and led him to a window. "Look out there," he said, pointing to the street. "What do you see?"

"I see men and women and little children," answered the rich man.

Again the rabbi took him by the hand and led him to the mirror and said, "What do you see now?"

"Now I see myself," the rich man replied.

Then the rabbi said, "Behold, in the window there is glass, but the glass of the mirror is covered with silver, and no sooner is the silver added than you fail to see others but see only yourself."

If you see self and all the respect and honor others ought to give you, you are on dangerous ground. Your eyesight will be dimmed. You won't be able to see others if self is the image you hold in front of you.

Wanting to Earn Our Own Salvation Can Blind Our Eyes to God's Provision in Christ

There is another thing that dims our eyesight. We cannot see what Jesus Christ can offer us if we want to have *a finger in our own salvation.* Two men were standing upon a bank fishing in water twenty feet deep. One man was an expert swimmer and the other could not swim at all. The man who could not swim lost his footing and fell into the water. He struggled to get out and tried to climb the slippery bank and fell back. A second time he rose, still struggling fiercely, while the man upon the bank looked calmly on with folded arms. At last the drowning man gave up hope and sank, helpless and exhausted. Then the man upon the bank dived into the water and lifted his friend out in safety and brought him back to life.

"Why didn't you save me before?" asked the man after he had regained consciousness.

"If I had attempted to save you at first," his friend answered, "when you were struggling, you would have caught me about the neck and we should both have been drowned. When you gave up, I could save you."

When we give up trying to save ourselves and trust Christ, He saves to the uttermost.

Self-Sufficiency a Form of Spiritual Blindness

Another blinding manifestation of self-seeking is when we magnify the ability of human nature, extolling the grandeur of our common humanity. How can a man who has his eyes upon self have any sight for Jesus? Are you trying to persuade others that you are self-sufficient, that you need nobody in your life? Be very careful. Of all anti-Christs, self is the hardest to overcome. It is written, "He must increase, but I must decrease" (John 3:30). But if proud self will not endure a decrease, how can you see Christ increasing?

Remember Mary Magdalene at the tomb of Christ? Having turned only partially, she had one eye upon the angels, and one eye upon the risen Christ. She mistook Him for the gardener instead of realizing that before her, beside her, stood the Lord. You cannot see the power of Christ's resurrection if your eyes are upon anybody to whom you attribute more honor than to Christ, whether they be saints or angels.

The Fear of Men a Hindrance to Clear Vision

The fear of men keeps many in darkness. If you hold to the faith once delivered to the saints, you will be considered old-fashioned. Can you make up your mind on your own, or do you depend upon the opinions of others? God has given to each individual an understanding, a personal light, which He expects us to use. Remember that even the leaders in whom you have placed your trust may be in darkness and cannot illumine your path. Oh, for a brighter spiritual eyesight!

Disobedience Destroys the Insight of the Soul

And the last thing that I want to mention that dims our spiritual eyesight is *disobedience*. To be faithless to the truth we apprehend is to put out, in some degree at least, the eyes of our understanding. The habitual denial of the will of God for the sake of interested and vicious motives destroys the insight of the soul and leaves us to stumble in the darkness. Our passions override our spiritual sensibilities; delicate nerves become unnourished, and transparent lenses are rendered opaque by disuse. Our utilitarian interests make us shortsighted. Our worldly life through the years spoils the eye which beholds God and the things of His Kingdom. The bright becomes indistinct. The great dwindles. The beautiful loses its magic.

There are those who have forfeited their noblest human heritage by repeated practical denials of the things which they have seen. Yes, even though they were not born without the faculty of seeing the invisible, the ego's eye has been quenched, being persistently turned toward things selfish, coarse, and unclean. And what we wish to recall here is that even partial disobedience means more or less of blindness. If you don't find in the Lord Jesus Christ what others find, don't blame Him. Blame yourself. Have you been obeying Christ? Are you acquainted with what He demands in your life through His Word?

What we must do if our intuitions are to be preserved clear, our sensibilities delicate, our wisdom large, is to pay an equal regard to all the requirements of God's Word. "Then shall I not be ashamed, when I have respect unto all thy commandments" (Ps. 119:6). Here the Psalmist touches the essential point. We are partial within ourselves, picking and choosing as to what we shall do and leave undone. Ready obedience to God's law in all its requirements, ready obedience to grace in all its impulses, these are the conditions of universal insight and wisdom.

> To keep thy conscience sensitive,
>   No inward token miss;
> And go where grace entices thee —
>   Perfection lies in this.
>   — Author Unknown

To see clearly, we must wish to see clearly. The number of beings who wish to see clearly is extraordinarily small. Startling but true! Men fail to see truly because they do not wish to see truly. It would cost too much. It would reveal a

81

path they are not prepared to follow. Pride, insincerity, self-will, spoil our perspicuity, make us incapable of appreciating the truth in its manifold aspects. A dark place develops in our heart and our love is chilled, a dark place in our understanding and our judgment is at fault, a dark place in our conscience and our conduct is wilting in consistency and blamelessness.

Living in the spirit of humility, sincerity, and obedience, we are sensitive to all the streaming light of Christ. Our soul is filled with its translucence, and every step of our pathway is irradiated by the bright shining of the candle of the Lord. Obedience is what makes our eyesight bright so we can see all the love and evotion of Jesus Christ. Obey, and all around and within you will glow with light.

THINK IT OVER

Here is a check list of things that can darken your spiritual vision. Rate yourself as honestly as you can in the column provided:

AM I GUILTY OF?   *NEVER SOMETIMES OFTEN*

1. Prejudice
2. Laziness
3. Gross doctrinal errors
4. Jealousy
5. Love of sin & pleasure
6. Greed
7. Pride
8. Egotism
9. Love of popularity and
     praise

10. Inordinate ambition
11. Salvation by works
12. Self-sufficiency
13. Fear of what men think of
    me
14. Disobedience to the known
    will of God

Note: It will be helpful to read over each section concerning these items before rating yourself.

9

The Necessity of a Balanced View of Divine Truth

Now, I want to discuss with you how the light may be perverted. Some people may have light enough; but their eye is in such evil condition that the light is turned into darkness. In the natural world, light could not actually become darkness, but in the spiritual world such a thing is possible. "When thine eye is evil," our Lord said, "thy body also is full of darkness. Take heed therefore that the light which is in thee be not darkness."

This is how the darkened mind thinks: "How can such a glorious Gospel be free? I must pay for it." Therefore it mixes a person's self-righteousness with the mercy of God. "If God is love and merciful, He will not punish anybody. Since God is gracious," the man with the darkened mind reasons, "let me live in sin. He will forgive me. He is a God of love. He will never allow anybody to suffer eternally. He'll give an opportunity to everybody to be saved."

That's how the light in a person is darkened. We need to examine our eyesight to determine whether we see all that there is to see in Jesus Christ. If anyone feels that there is a chance of salvation after death, of doing it over, there is something wrong with his eyesight.

Don't Limit God by Over-Emphasis on a Particular Doctrine

Some born-again Christians who believe in the Word of God, have certain blind spots of doctrine in their hearts. The doctrine may be correct, but it is stressed out of proportion to the other doctrines of the Word of God. They may see in Christ only a stern sovereign God without flexibility or mercy. But even a cursory reading of the Gospels will show Jesus Christ to be full of mercy and of justice as well. A balanced view of God, a balanced view of the Bible, a balanced view of Jesus Christ, is obtained only with balanced spiritual eyesight. Some people, of course, are totally blind as far as spiritual truth is concerned. But among believers there are many who see only imperfectly, intermittently, and partially.

The Partial Appreciation of Divine Truth

Let's consider this matter of the partial appreciation of divine truth. Christian people, who in the main are very good and wise, sometimes startle us by their inadequate knowledge of Jesus Christ. We see this limitation, for instance, with regard to the doctrine of the sovereignty of God, the divine government. They see in God only an arbitrary dictator who sets His own course and is unmoved by the pleas of His people. This is wrong. God is stern, indeed, but He loves and listens to His people and is concerned with their plight.

There are others whose view of their own church is greatly distorted. They believe it is the only true church, and anybody who does not belong to their own denomination or church cannot belong to Jesus Christ. They take the position, "If you are not of us, you are not of Christ."

Pharisaical Pride Limits Christian Fellowship

Oh, my friends, these dark spots in our hearts can bring division and bitterness, can put us out of fellowship with wonderful Christians who may belong to some other church than ours. We may be depriving ourselves of precious fellowship by believing that we can fellowship only with those who belong to our own denominational group.

If that's your case, you are losing a great deal. There is a dark spot in your eyesight, in your heart, in your view of God. Expand that view. Become a farsighted Christian instead of a nearsighted Pharisee.

An unknown poet penned these lines that describe the person who makes himself the sole authority of divine truth:

> Believe as I believe, no more, no less;
> That I am right, and no one else, confess;
> Feel as I feel, think only as I think;
> Eat what I eat, and drink but what I drink;
> Look as I look, do always as I do;
> And then, and only then, I'll fellowship
>   with you.
>
> That I am right, and always right, I know,
> Because my own convictions tell me so;
> And to be right is simply this — to be
> Entirely and in all respects like me;
> To deviate a hair's breadth, or begin
> To question, or to doubt, or hesitate, is
>   sin.
>
> I reverence the Bible if it be
> Translated first, and then explained by me;

87

By churchly laws and customs I abide
If they with my opinion coincide;
All creeds and doctrines I concede divine,
Excepting those, of course, that disagree
with mine.

*   *   *   *   *   *   *

'Twere better sinners perish than refuse
To be conformed to my peculiar views;
'Twere better that the world stand still,
than move
In any other way than that which I approve.

Do you know any individuals like that? Do you secretly entertain a similar attitude yourself at times? Watch out for Pharisaism.

Don't Limit God in the Matter of Baptism

There are others, for instance, who overemphasize the doctrine of baptism, believing that a person cannot be a Christian unless he is baptized in their own group and by their own ministers. If that were true, then Jesus Christ did not tell the truth to the thief on the cross when He said, "To day shalt thou be with me in paradise" (Luke 23:43). The thief had no chance of being baptized, yet he was going to be with Jesus Christ in paradise.

Baptism in its outward form is only an expression of our death, burial, and resurrection with Jesus Christ; but the physical act is not the most important thing. We observe it in obedience to Jesus Christ, and as a demonstration to the outside world of what has happened to us spiritually. But let's not place such importance on the outward physical rite that we deprive the spiritual experience of its importance. Watch out for overemphasis on a particular doctrine with which some other Christians may differ. We must be extremely careful lest we limit God.

Beware of "Tunnel Vision"

Take the Puritan doctrine, for instance. There are some people today who won't read anything but Puritan writers, as if modern writers and preachers who lived after the Puritan era have had nothing to offer to the understanding of the Word of God. The Puritans had their times, and today theologians and Bible teachers have their own time. Have an enlarged view of the spectrum of Christian history with regard to the Word of God, and of Christ as having different members in His body, all of whom must appreciate one another. The hand, the foot must appreciate the guidance of the eye and ear to avoid danger. We are to work together. Have no blind spot in your heart, the Lord warns. "Take heed therefore that the light which is in thee be not darkness." Jesus Christ is this light; it is His Gospel, it is His saving grace; watch out lest the light that is in you may be darkened by tunnel vision that can see only what it wants to see.

There is also a misconception about the duty that we have toward God and our fellow believers. Some people insist on their own mode of serving Christ as the only indicator of faithfulness to God. We must not do this. God may be served by others in a different manner than you and I are serving Him. You know, it is perilously easy to recognize the obligation and delight of one phase of duty, while being comparatively blind to another phase equally imperative and delightful. The unequally gifted artist makes a good sculptor but a bad painter, and Christian men and women who are shining examples in one direction are often painful failures in another. We must appreciate the manner in which other people serve Christ, even if that manner is different from ours. Do not have a dark spot in your heart concerning duty.

The same thing may be said of the Supper of the Lord. Some people believe that the bread is so sanctified, the grape juice is so sanctified, that they are actually holy. No, it is what they symbolize that is sacred, the body and the blood of our Savior, broken and shed for our sins.

There are some people who substitute public worship for inward forgiveness of sin and holiness of life. They believe that going to church is the essential element of a good life, without realizing that it is not one's physical presence in church that counts, but one's spiritual communion with God there.

The Danger of Accepting Exterior Substitutes for the Interior Function of the Holy Spirit

We have blind spots in our hearts, when we substitute something exterior for the importance of the interior function of the Holy Spirit within us. Some people look upon church membership as a certificate of salvation. It is not. Membership in the body of Christ by faith in Jesus Christ is what is important. Some consider baptism as the door into the Kingdom of God, instead of a living faith in the atoning work of Christ. It never says in Scripture that those who are not baptized are going to hell, are condemned, but it says "they that believe not" (John 3:18).

Faith is the important thing. Faith is what introduces us into the body of Christ, not the admission into a local body of believers, although that is very essential to spiritual growth and fellowship. Everyone must have a house in which to live, so to speak. Yes, we must belong to a local church that preaches the Gospel, but belonging to Jesus Christ first of all is the important thing.

Be Careful that Religious Symbols Do Not Degenerate into Superstitions

When instructive symbols are perverted into instruments of priestcraft, the light that is within us is turned into darkness. Aids to faith are often degraded into the machinery of superstition. The Church, which is our mother and nurse, is made into an antichrist, and men look to her for salvation instead of looking to Jesus Christ alone. Let us never consider any human being, be he priest or bishop, minister or pastor, as more important to us than our own Lord Jesus Christ who has saved us from sin. Don't deify the church, don't deify the ministers or the priests. But remember, Jesus Christ stands above all. Outward modes of instruction and worship may be very helpful. They may be a means of bringing us closer to God, but they are never the end in themselves. If they are allowed to usurp the confidence of the soul they may produce disease and death.

It is possible, then, for a man's religion, if it becomes a religion of types and formalities and rites, to become his destruction. It is possible for his own religion to become the dark spot in his heart.

Sincerity Not Enough

Our light becomes darkness when we believe that a sincere spirit is everything, regardless of the content of our belief. We grow indifferent in doctrine and licentious in life. We conclude that there is some measure of truth in everything, and that every evil practice has some good point about it. This is a poisonous atmosphere for any man to breathe. He rejects absolute truth and assigns relativity to everything. Such a person is like a chameleon which takes its color from the changing light about it. We can so easily call something

91

"liberty" which is really "indifference." We may say, "I'm free to go to prayer meeting or not; I'm free to go to church or not," and we are really trying to excuse our indifference by attributing it to our liberty in Christ. That's a dark spot in our enlightened heart.

Or we neglect to help the poor, and we claim that we are free to follow our conscience in this matter, yet all the while we are merely excusing our indifference.

A student may turn his light into darkness by starting to be critical, first with the things that may be criticized, and then proceed to belittle those things that are beyond criticism. He is like a little boy with a new knife; he must cut something or other. He cuts up the Scriptures and decimates them; he has such a sharp knife that he must use it or otherwise he is not happy. From a critic, he advances to an irreverent faultfinder, and from that to an utter unbeliever. His light has blinded him.

Our light may be perverted through the loss of the full assurance of our faith. Assurance, however, must never be counterfeited by presumption. We must never take for granted that we are children of God, without Scriptural warrant for it, or assume the appropriation of privileges that are not ours.

THINK IT OVER

1. Have you known Christians who believe the Word of God, but who emphasize one or more doctrines out of proportion to, or even to the neglect of other doctrines of the Bible?
2. Have you a "pet doctrine" that you harp on or argue about, so that you lack a balanced view of all the other doctrines of God's Word?

3. Do you lack a spirit of unity with believers in other Bible-preaching churches because they differ with your own denomination in some particular not essential to salvation?

4. Have you put God "in a box" by saying He cannot bless others outside the context of your understanding of Scripture? (See Matt. 5:44-48.)

10

The Results of Defective Spiritual Vision

When there is defective enlightenment in the heart, certain evil consequences follow. Defective enlightenment destroys that perfect peace which is the privilege of God's children.

We sometimes say, "What the eye does not see the heart does not grieve for," but that is not true here. Ignorance, error, and the faults that spring from them mean restlessness, discontentment, and sorrow. It is not only our positive obvious defects that breed misery. Far more than we think, the hidden things of the heart are what determine the brightness or the sadness of our experience. There is no greater joy than to walk in the truth, and every whit that we fall short of the truth implies that we fall equally short of full felicity.

It is said that spots upon the sun indicate terrestrial confusion and disaster; similarly the dark places of the soul indicate smitten and withered spaces in our thought and experience. We ask in perplexity, "Why art thou cast down, O my soul? and why art thou disquieted within me?" (Ps. 42:5). But if we could trace many of our real, yet vague, experiences of wretchedness to their obscure origin, we should find that they come from those places in our heart where the light does not shine.

Defective Spiritual Vision Results in a Deformed Character

Secondly, another evil that results from our defective enlightenment is that our character is maimed. Some time ago we noticed a tree planted at the sunny end of a house, and there the blossoms were large and beautiful. It was a feast to the eyes; but some of the branches were trained round the corner of the house, where they got much less sun, and the difference was amazing. The blossoms were starved and drooping, and there was little promise of fruit. They had the same root and stem in common, but while one part of the tree was in the full glorious light, the other branches were in the shade.

It is thus in character. The dark places mean unfruitful branches, strange weaknesses, distortions, immaturities, indirection, failures in practical life and conduct. "The fruit of the Spirit is love, joy, peace, longsuffering, gentleness, goodness, faith, meekness, temperance" (Gal. 5:22, 23). And if we are to bear all manner of precious fruit, each in its rightful season, we must trustfully and joyfully lay open our whole soul to the full noon of God's light shining in the face of Jesus Christ.

Defective Spiritual Vision a Source of Peril to the Soul

The third evil that the blind spot causes, besides destroying peace and maiming character, is that it lays us open to peril.

Here where our mind is confused, our conscience hesitating, our feeling morbid, our will inoperative, the great danger of life lies. In the human eye there is a spot where the optic nerve enters, which is known as the blind spot. Cricketers talk a great deal about this visual imperfection, for sooner or later the bowler finds out the blind spot, the batsman misjudges the ball, and his sport comes to an end.

The devil plays for the blind spot, and if there is such a defect in our spirit, sooner or later he brings us into trouble. The blind spot in the natural eye is a necessary, unavoidable, physiological defect of which the brightest and most skillful athlete cannot rid himself; but morally and religiously no part of our nature need be dark, and we may successfully defend ourselves in every assault. If for any subtle self-serving we allow some bias of the mind, some prejudice that warps the judgment, some neglect of charity, some inertia that obstructs conviction, some deviation of aim, some deflection in action, we lay ourselves open to grievous losses and sorrows. "But if we walk in the light, as he [God] is in the light, we have fellowship one with another" (I John 1:7).

If we don't have fellowship with other believers, there is a dark spot in our eyesight. The Christian whose heart is full of light enjoys the company of those of like precious faith. "And the blood of Jesus Christ his Son cleanseth us from all sin." It is our privilege to walk in the full light, to have our whole soul instructed and luminous.

There is in nature a mollusk with 11,000 eyes, and as the shell grows the eyes still multiply. Surely, men ought to be full of eyes of inspirations, perceptions, sensibilities, so that they might realize truly and happily the vast bright universe of which they are the heirs. Let us be sure that while Christ promised to us the Spirit who should guide us into the whole truth, we do not come short of appropriating His gracious promise.

God's Word Our Standard and Source of Clear Spiritual Vision

Take heed, therefore, take heed to God's Word. To see clearly we must test and strengthen our vision by revelation. "To the law and to the testimony: if they speak not according to this word, it is because there is no light in them" (Isa. 8:20). How impossible it is to express the value of this standard and source of vision. "What advantage then hath the Jew? . . . Much every way: chiefly, because that unto them were committed the oracles of God" (Romans 3:1, 2). With diseased organs of sight, perplexed by dark and dancing shadows, it is a peculiarly precious thing to have this master light of all our seeing.

By the aid of that most perfect scientific instrument the ophthalmoscope, with its condensing mirror and myriad of little lenses, the ophthalmologist can look into a person's eye and see spread before him a record of the action of many of the more important organs of the human body. Not only is he by this means able to determine approximately the necessary strength of glass required to give perfect vision, but also the existence of tumors pressing on the brain tissue, the condition of the general nervous system, the presence of disease in various organs, and the richness of the blood current as they are clearly traced on the sensitive plate of nature's camera.

What the ophthalmoscope is to the ophthalmologist, enabling him to see the defects of the eye and obscure defects of the system that the eye may indicate, revelation is to a higher nature a test and criticism of supreme value. One of the ways by which we can prevent this darkening of our eyesight is to look daily at the Word of God, so that the Word may become the mirror to which we are exposed. "The word of God is quick, and powerful, and sharper than any two-edged sword, piercing even to the dividing asunder of soul and spirit, and of the joints and marrow, and is a discerner of the thoughts and intents of the heart" (Heb. 4:12). If we wish to see clearly, we must test and purge our vision. Here is the radical cure for spiritual cataract and colorblindness. To see truly we must see light in God's light. After the dust and fog and mirage of a day that we have lived in our town or city, it is a wonderful restorative to cleanse the eyes with the eyesalve of the Word of God.

We must take heed to our spirit and life. To see it truly we must keep our soul in health. Our general health often determines our physical vision. If with our bodily eyes we are to see at our best, we must decline the things that adversely affect our total health. We must abstain from intemperance, live in purity, maintain our strength and vigor. Seeing clearly is not a matter that stands apart from our general health, but it is the sign and consequence of bodily perfection.

True Seeing Is the Result of True Living

It is thus, too, with our superior nature. We must keep the soul in health if we are to see things as God sees them. The luster of the eye is dependent upon the purity of the heart. True seeing is the reward of true living. Most precious and blessed is that spiritual faculty by which we see the realities of the eternal world, that moral sense by which we discern the beauty and obligation of the law of righteousness, that moral sympathy which puts us into fellowship with the living God. "And this I pray, that your love may abound yet more and more in knowledge and in all judgment; that ye may approve things that are excellent; that ye may be sincere and without offence till the day of Christ; being filled with the fruits of righteousness, which are by Jesus Christ, unto the glory and praise of God" (Phil. 1:9-11).

The Worst Effect of Defective Spiritual Vision — Loss of Godly Fear

So, we have seen thus far that the black spots in our hearts can destroy our peace, they can maim our character, they imply peril. But, the worst thing that can happen is that a dark spot in our hearts may pervert us so that we lose our holy fear. It is the light that comes from God that makes a man afraid to sin, so that he fears lest he should grieve the Spirit of God, and trembles lest in anything he should depart from the teaching of the Father. But this light may be corrupted into slavish dread, despondency, and despair. Fear that is holy does not lead to despondency but to dependency upon God and the truth of His promises. Our Lord said, "If therefore the light that is in thee be darkness, how great is that darkness!" (Matt. 6:23). What He meant is, If that which should lead you actually misleads you, how misled you will be! If your better part turns out to be evil, how evil you must be. Let us be sure that we have a clear eye and that the light of Christ comes streaming into our souls in all its glorious purity and power — and that can be done only as we expose ourselves constantly to the light of the Word of God.

THINK IT OVER

1. What is the cause of a lack of peace in the heart, a crippled character, defeat when tempted by Satan, and loss of holy fear of God so that a Christian is not afraid to sin?
2. How and where can the believer find the remedy for these spiritual defects?
3. Do you ever suffer from depression of soul? If so, read Psalms 42 and 43 for renewal of faith.

11

The Action of Light
When It Enters the Soul

How does the light act when it comes within the soul? If the eye is bright, "single," as the Word of God tells us, and clear, the eye does not have to do any strenuous work to obtain the light. When the sun is shining, if we wish for light we simply open our eyes and we have light at once. When the eye is sound, it takes pleasure in the light, and with delight conveys the image of things external to the mind within. If the Lord in His great grace has made our eye single so that we desire to know only the truth and to be true ourselves, then without toil we will perceive truth, and its image will readily appear before our minds.

The First Entrance of Light to Our Souls Reveals Hidden Sins

The light is willing enough to enter when the window of the soul allows its admission. When that light comes in, we'll know it. No man passes from his natural darkness into heavenly light without being aware that a great change has taken place. When the light first comes in, it reveals much that before was unperceived. If a room has been shut for a long time and kept in darkness, the light has a startling effect. With the light of a candle we cannot detect the dust, but if we open the shutters and draw the blinds, the light makes the mold and the dust very apparent. The light of heaven reveals a thousand sins, and causes their removal.

The first effect of the light of God in the soul is painfully unpleasant. It makes us loathe ourselves and wish we had never been born. Things grow worse and worse to our consciences as the light shines more and more. We would have every part of us opened to the light. We would have every idol discovered and broken, and every dark chamber exposed to the sun. We must not keep the light out of any part of our nature. The light should be permitted to continue to enter our souls, and as it does, it gradually illuminates. Our will by nature prefers the darkness. It claims the right to act as we please. The light must continue to enter if our will is going to be made willing to change.

The Effect of Light Is Seen in an Enlightened Conscience

The light enlightens the conscience. We may be living unconsciously in evils for which our conscience has never once accused us. For instance, I know a woman who is deeply spiritual, but there is a dark spot in her conscience. At work, she loves to carry on conversations with others, allowing her work to suffer. This is stealing. But our conscience may never realize that, when we talk about our private affairs during working hours, that is a form of stealing. There is a black spot on our conscience and we have never before perceived the evil of it. As the light continues to enter, it illumines our motives and unveils the secret heart of all our actions.

The Light Reveals the Evil Imaginations of the Heart

As the light continues to enter, it illumines our imagination. In the dark chambers of imagination, the heart commits murders, adulteries, thefts, and all kinds of sin. When the light falls here, we shudder as we learn that as we think in our hearts so are we. We tremble as we perceive the deformed imagination of sin is actually sin.

We need this light to shine also upon our tempers. Some take license to be as surly as they like on the grounds of, "Well, it's my constitution; I can't help it. I'm made that way." They blame it on hereditary traits. We cannot carry a bad temper into heaven. Our desires, hopes, fears, aspirations should continue to have the light of Christ shine upon them. If we are in a dark place we don't know what's around us. We are possessed with fear. But if we have light we have assurance and certainty; we are grounded; and that's what the Lord Jesus Christ does for us when He comes into our hearts.

Light Brings Assurance and a Sense of Direction

Nothing disqualifies us for doing God's work more than a doubt, as to our salvation, for instance. Mr. Moody used to illustrate this by saying: "If I were in the river, and I didn't have a firm grip on something, I couldn't help anybody. I've got to get a good hold for myself before I can help someone else." There is no liberty, peace, rest, joy, or power until we have assurance.

Do you have that assurance? Do you have that certainty that you are saved and that the light of Jesus Christ is flooding your soul? With this spirit of assurance comes direction. Otherwise how would we know where to go? We can see our way and how to walk in it.

103

The Light Reveals Christ as Our Supreme Source of Joy

The light of Jesus Christ when He dwells in the heart also brings good cheer with it — joy — and joy is one of the greatest elements of life in the Christian walk.

A certain king instructed his gardener to plant six trees and place statues beneath them representing prosperity, beauty, victory, strength, duty, and joy. These trees were to show to the world that the king had tried to make his reign fruitful. They were also to typify the statues beneath them. The gardener planted six palm trees. When the king came out to inspect the work and looked at the statue of joy, he said, "I surely thought you would typify joy with some flowering tree like the tulip or magnolia. How can the stately palm symbolize joy?"

"Those trees," said the gardener, "get their happiness from manifest and open sources. They live in merry forests or orchards with hosts of happy comrades. But I found this palm tree in a sandy waste. Its roots had found some hidden spring creeping along far beneath the burning surface. Then, thought I, the highest joy has a foundation unseen of men and a source they cannot comprehend."

Do you realize that if the light of Jesus Christ is within your heart it can be the only place in which joy is found, and yet it will be sufficient. You do not need the company of others in order to experience the joy that the light of Christ brings. A palm tree does not need the company of other trees to flourish and bring forth fruit.

Darkness is doleful; light brings delight. Our Lord added, "If the whole body therefore be full of light, having no part dark, the whole shall be full of light" (Luke 11:36). He compares our inward light to a candle that shines upon us and our surroundings. When a room is well lighted in every

104

corner, it has a joyous splendor. We look about and feel content and satisfied. So when the whole nature is full of the light of God, we have sweetness and light to the full, and heaven seems to have begun below.

The Inner Sight Radiates to Bring Blessing to Others

There should therefore be no concealment and no love of evil. This inner light will make us shine before others. It is the only shining we should seek. A clean lantern with a lighted candle in it makes no noise and yet it wins attention. We don't have to make noise if Jesus Christ is in our hearts. His light shines forth, and others are looking at it. It becomes a guiding star to them. The darker the night, the more it is valued.

There was never a time in which true inner light was more needed than now. May the Lord impart it to each one of us, so that we shall shine as lights in the world. We don't have to work for the light, we only have to receive it. Let us keep our lamp trimmed and the lamp will shine brilliantly, bringing direction, peace, certainty, and cheer, not only to ourselves but also to others. Our character will profit by the light that is in us and the world will know it.

THINK IT OVER

1. How has the light of God's Word affected you personally in the following areas:
   a. Your recognition of previously hidden sins?
   b. Your conscience, as to what it will or will not permit you to do?
   c. Your assurance of salvation?

2. How does assurance give you a sense of direction as to the aims and ideals that should govern your life?
3. How can the light within you become a blessing to others?

12

Determining Life's Meaning
and Our Own Ideals in Consequence

In Luke 11:35 our Lord says, "Take heed therefore that the light which is in thee be not darkness." But the Greek word for "take heed" is not really translated correctly. It is *skopei,* which is better translated "keep looking." It is from the word *skopeoo* of which the noun is *skopos,* from which we derive the word *episkopos,* "bishop." It means "oversee." "Oversee, keep looking, therefore, whether perhaps the light, the one in thee, is darkness." That is the literal translation of this verse. In other words, we must keep constant watch over the light that has come to us from Jesus Christ. It is possible to have that light of Christ in us, yet for us to show to the world that we are still in darkness.

When people look at us, is there light in us? Or are we dark? We've got to watch it. We are constantly to look at the eye or the light that it permits to enter. You see, the eye is our faith, faith that permits the light of Christ to come into us. Everything depends on what we permit our eye to look at.

The Tragedy of Possessing Light That Produces No Illumination in a Sinful World

Now if the light in us becomes darkness, it is not the fault of that light, but of how we have treated God's light in us. You remember that our Lord said it is possible for us to light a candle and put it under a bushel, to put it in a dark place, to cover it up. Therefore, although there is light, there is no illumination shed around. And that's what's happening in the world today. There are a great many Christians, but there is little illumination in the world. What has happened to our light within us? We must be careful lest it has become darkness. There is no witness, there is no shining forth of the Spirit of Christ.

Facing the Fact That It Is Possible for the Believer, the Enlightened One, To Sin

Now, the word darkness means "sin" here. Note two Greek words: *skotos*, which means darkness symbolic of sin, and the diminitive word *skotia*, which means the result of sin. What our Lord is saying here is, "Take heed, watch it, constantly oversee your lives lest the light, the one that is in you, the light that you have appropriated in you, becomes darkness, becomes sin." Scripture clearly indicates that it is possible for the believer, the one who has permitted the light of the Word of God, the light of Christ, to come into him, to sin. We should not sin, we should be holy in our lives. But facts are facts, and of course there are degrees of sinfulness.

When I speak of sin, I do not mean that the believer will go out and kill somebody, or steal, although unfortunately that can happen. I am referring to sin as James 4:17 defines it: "Therefore to him that knoweth to do good, and doeth it not, to him it is sin." Do you realize, for instance, that if it is within your power to help somebody in need today, and you do not

108

do it, it is a sin? It is a dark spot in you. It is possible for the light of Jesus Christ to be within us and yet for us to have dark spots, sins. The holier we become the more we realize the sinfulness of sin.

The Danger of Saying, "Everybody Does It, So That's Not Sin"

For instance, take two workmen. One of them just fools around in the work that he is paid for, and thinks nothing of it. Why, who cares? The other person, who is conscientious and works diligently and well, is one who cares. Both are Christians. What makes the difference? One has a consciousness of the sinfulness of sin, while the other looks at sin with darkened eyes and says, "That's not sin. Everybody does it. Why shouldn't I do it? Why shouldn't I collect unemployment while I can, instead of going out to look for work?" That's stealing the labor of somebody else. He is lazy, he allows somebody else to work, and while he is not working he is collecting the fruit of the labor of somebody else.

When we lose our ability to evaluate the sinfulness of sin, there is darkness within our souls. That's what we have here as the teaching of our Lord. It is possible for Jesus Christ, the light of the world, to be within our souls, and yet for us to have dark spots in our life. We must keep constant watch over our inner life. We can never sit down and say, "I have now arrived."

Do Others See Light or Darkness as They Evaluate Your Life as a Christian?

That's what the teaching is here. It is possible, our Lord tells us, to have the light of the world within us and yet for the world to look at us and see darkness. In other words, there is danger that our ideals may not shine forth and become examples to others. We must guard constantly against the light that is within us becoming darkness.

We do not need to be informed of course as to the use of the eye, because for all practical purposes we know what it is. The value of the sense of sight, however, can only be fully appreciated by those who have been deprived of it. It is the lamp of the body because it enables us to regulate and direct our activities to the greatest advantage and with the least possible danger. It shows us where to go and where not to venture, what to do and what to leave undone — to say nothing of the exquisite loveliness or form of light and shade, of ever-varying tint and all the color schemes that the eye makes possible as the organ of vision.

How and What We See Determine Our True Destiny for Good or Ill

In order that sight may be normal, two main conditions are essential. Both eyes must be in good working order in order to have binocular vision instead of skopic effect. Also, it is necessary that there should be objects presented to consciousness through the retina, and these objects must be presented through the medium of light. We have here, as in all conscious states, the twofold element of the subjective and the objective.

Transfer this to the spiritual plane and we shall then see how our Master's teaching applies. In order that we may direct our lives to the best effect, and in view of the objects for which we have been endowed with life — in other words, if we are to find our true destiny, and order all our activities intelligently and well — we need the two elements, the organ of spiritual vision and, no less, the illumined object of that vision. The eye must not be a bad or faulty eye, or darkness may result from the soul's defective vision. Again it is possible to follow wrongly illuminated objects and the light may play us false. Not only are we in the dark when the soul's vision is dulled and obscured, but it is even more distressing when the guiding principles of our life are perverted. This is what our Lord meant by our light becoming darkness, that the principles that guide us become perverted, defective. If the guiding light is misleading and we follow the half light, or if, so to speak, the lighthouses and lightships are misplaced and give the wrong signals, we are worse off than if we had no light at all. If the light that is in us is darkness, how great is that darkness!

Determining Life's Meaning and Our Own Ideals

It is quite clear that in the ordering and shaping of our lives and in directing our activities, we need an aim, a goal, an objective. What do we live for? What are we working for? And what is the ultimate for which we strive? Life cannot possibly be a success if it is allowed to drift on aimlessly. It is not a mere idle stroll or an aimless cruise. We need to know the object of all endeavor and the way in which that object is to be achieved. We speak of it as life's meaning or purpose when we are considering the final cause, but we term it our ideal when it refers to personal achievement and character and the realized self.

Why is it worthwhile to be good, to love and appreciate the beautiful, and to gain the truth? It is because these objects are of value in themselves and because they ultimately center in Him who is the only proper object for all human endeavor, and because in the acceptance of Christ as the soul's great objective, we come to live in the light. As John said, "Coming into the world, He was the light, the true one, which keeps illuminating every man" (John 1:9, author's translation).

The eye of the soul is the function of faith that directs our whole being towards Him, the supreme object in reality that gives meaning and force to our whole vital activities. Every man must have an ideal of some sort, and I suppose that every man has. It is that which inspires him to act and that shapes his destiny and directs his vital energies, be it good or bad, indifferent, or defective. The ideal makes him what he is, and no man is better than his ideal, although he is better than he ever could be without it. So far as it is presented and apprehended by him, that ideal must be right and good, for if it is distorted, one-sided, or badly balanced, and especially if it is false, the man's whole life will be subject to delusion, distortion, and defect. It is a case of the light that is within him becoming darkness.

The Peril of Compromising Our Ideals for Lesser Gains

Perhaps the most seductive of all evil influence and darkness in the soul, in the perversion of the ideal, is to make what ought to be the ultimate aim and ends in themselves subordinate to other considerations. We shall all readily admit that no artist ever does his best or most inspiring work who holds fame and influence to be higher than the beautiful that he endeavors to interpret through the medium of his own personality. The best work is never done merely for gain.

But how often we have been at fault in our thinking and advice in recommending religion as a means to an end, to make the best of both worlds, rather than as the end in itself. Any kind of recommendation that is put forward for religion as the means to advancement, or to make life comfortable or pleasant, or even to gain heaven or escape hell, is certain to bring about incalculable mischief, for the reason that true religion can never be the means to any other end. Such teaching may attract selfish people for prudent reasons, and all who set the highest value upon personal safety and happiness, but it will inevitably deter those whom it is of the utmost importance to win. Besides this, it will surely come to pass that, if the means are no longer successful, they will be set aside in order that the ends in view may not be lost. Let us be careful not to make the means the ends in our life. Let us have an ideal, and let Christ be that ideal. Let Him not become darkened in any way.

THINK IT OVER

1. What is the great tragedy of Christendom today with regard to the light of the Gospel?
2. Name the two classes of sin to which the believer is subject because of his "old nature." (See James 4:17 and Psalm 19:13.)
3. If otherwise good-living Christians indulge in "borderline practices," does that tempt you to use their example as an excuse to do likewise?
4. They say "Every man has his price." What is your weak point that Satan could use to tempt you from doing your best for Christ?

13

Freedom of Conscience as Taught by Christ

The Lord Jesus was considered an extremely dangerous teacher by His contemporaries, especially the ecclesiastical hierarchy, though "the common people heard him gladly." He was put to death on the charge, among others, of perverting the nation and leading men astray. It may be difficult for us to understand how any such charge could have been brought against Him, and more difficult still to explain how it could have been upheld in a legal trial. That, of course, is because we inherit nearly two thousand years of Christian teaching and we came into a world dominated to some extent by the teaching and ideals of Jesus. Our thoughts about Him have been molded and fashioned for us so that we find a real difficulty in seeing Christ as His contemporaries, the Pharisees and scribes, saw Him.

But if we had lived when He was teaching, we would have been in an entirely different position. Our ways of thought would have been different. We would have had other ideals, and our reaction to His teaching would not have been what it is today. Many things would have struck us as very dangerous if not revolutionary. And one of these would have been His insistence that men should have the privilege of private judgment.

The Right of Private Judgment a Basic and Radical Teaching of Christ

Do you realize that this is basic to the religion of Jesus Christ? He gives us the privilege of private judgment. He says in effect, "Here is what will change your life, but it will only do so if you accept it." That's private judgment. That's a decision that each individual must make. For instance, our Lord did not prescribe that men should pray five times a day as Mohammed did to the Moslems. He taught that people should be in constant communion with God. He prescribed no external act of worship, but taught a spiritual relationship. That is the religion of Christ — a religion of conscience.

It was courageous in those days to suggest that men should exercise private judgment in the affairs of life. No one did so, not even the rabbis, the teachers themselves. These learned men would never have dared to determine any moral issue on their own authority. No rabbi considered his own personal opinion on matters of life and conduct authoritative.

One of the great contrasts between the Lord Jesus and these Jewish teachers, a contrast that greatly impressed the people, was that while they would never decide a moral issue on their own authority, the Lord Jesus always did so. He didn't say, "Just do this, that, or the other thing," but presented a decision that the individual must come to on his own. The Lord Jesus exercised private understanding, con-science, and decision. He always allowed His own conscience to decide the issue and determine His choice.

But the people of that day wouldn't dare to exercise

116

personal judgment. They fell back on the traditions and judgments of the past for their authority, very much as we do today in our law courts when some point of law is in dispute. In such a case, it is not then a question of what opposing council thinks. The point raised can only be settled by reference to some accepted authority, probably the decision of a famous judge in a similar case.

Traditional Authority the Norm in Jesus' Day

This was the attitude the Jewish teachers adopted in their differences of opinion and interpretation. They did not express what they personally believed to be right or wrong. They sought some source of authority, some outstanding teacher of the past with regard to the position they adopted. This is why they made reference to Abraham. "Abraham believed this, and you say this," was their rebuttal of Christ's teaching. It was distinction, or weight of authority, that ultimately decided the point at issue.

Jesus never adopted this method of teaching or judging moral issues, and people were quick to discern it. He exercised His own private judgment and relied upon His own moral standards for guidance. That is why the people said of Him, "He teaches as one having authority, and not as the scribes," who never claimed authority for themselves. (See Matt. 7:29 & Mark 1:22.)

This was one of the features of Christ's public ministry that seemed extremely dangerous to the Jewish leaders. They could not be reconciled to it, and were vocally intolerant in their attitude towards it. They considered it especially dangerous when the Lord Jesus was prepared to extend the same privilege to the common crowd, those people who were accursed because they knew not the Law. They saw nothing but chaos and ruin, confusion and destruction, in the individual conscience. The Lord Jesus transgressed all their canons of teaching when He claimed to be His own authority. And He outraged their common sense when He was prepared to allow ordinary people to judge for themselves.

"Think for Yourselves"—Jesus' Advice to the Multitudes

Yet, this is what He did. He advised people to exercise a right and privilege of personal and private judgment. "Yea, and why even of yourselves judge ye not what is right?" (Luke 12:57), was the pointed question that He put to them. Use your own judgment. Exercise your own conscience. Trust your own sense of right and wrong. Think for yourselves. Judge for yourselves. Let your decisions, your moral choices, be your own.

The Lord Jesus took this position and never departed from it, and we, of course, have followed Him in this and have claimed for ourselves the privilege and right of private judgment. We allow our conscience to determine our moral choices and to guide us in all our ways. Now, the Lord Jesus allows us this liberty. He sets forth a moral precept and tells us we may decide to do it, or we may decide not to do it. But He always sets forth the consequences of our choice. In other words, He would say, "If you read a book that has low moral standards, you will become degraded yourself." He always declares the consequences of our choice, but He leaves the choice to us.

Freedom of Conscience Is Not License

Jesus did not leave the matter there and neither should we. There is something more to be said, and nobody has said it more plainly or more forcibly than He. Jesus never made a fetish of conscience as many of us do, nor did He interpret freedom of conscience in terms of license. Yes, there are perils connected with conscience and the privilege of private judgment. The light that is in us may become darkness. The Lord Jesus, in giving us the privilege of private judgment, did not tell us what to do in every decision we would be called upon to make: whether to smoke or not to smoke, how many hours to work, how much to give to the Lord's work, and so on. But He gave us basic principles to guide us in exercising the privilege of private judgment. Today some Christians feel free to do certain things that other Christians do not do. Conscience is the thing that governs us. But we must be careful lest we abuse freedom of conscience by thinking of it in terms of license to do as we please.

Legalistic Christianity Is a Form of Slavery

We know, of course, what can be said in favor of the individual conscience. It is wonderful to have this freedom; there is no more miserable Christianity than legalistic Christianity. Do this, do that, your dress should be up to a certain point of the leg, not one single inch above or below. Legalism is slavery. We know that the exercise of freedom of conscience is the only way in which a sense of right and wrong can be developed. We realize that their way of denying the right of private judgment is where the Lord clashed with the scribes and the Pharisees of His day. They wanted to adhere to the letter of the Law, allowing no private judgment. We realize that this resulted in the end in atrophied and petrified moral powers. Where conscience is not exercised it ceases to function. It simply dies out of life, and in that case our loss is greater than we can know, because we have been cut away from the root of progress.

The Privilege of Freedom of Conscience Is Linked with Responsibility.

It is essential that we should exercise conscience, but let us not forget, what we are all apt to forget, that in this matter as in all others, privilege is linked with responsibility. If we claim the right to exercise our individual conscience, let us not regard it as a toy to be played with. It is a weapon whose use can bring destruction, not only to ourselves but to others. There are great dangers associated with this privilege, and that is where our responsibility begins. It is a good thing to look not only at the privilege but at the responsibility as well.

Probably it is this aspect of conscience that makes religious leaders at times hesitate to commend it as a guide of life. For the great Jewish church was not the only one to refuse to individuals this right of conscience. Some powerful churches today have adopted the same attitude. Some priests, some ministers, some churches tell people what to do in every circumstance. The communicants of these legalistic congregations must not consult their own moral sense to decide the moral issues of their individual lives. They must ascertain what the church, through its priests and teachers, says, and by that they must be guided in all things.

The Perils of Freedom of Choice

This is not the Gospel of Christ. We are permitted to exercise our privilege of private judgment. Of course, we may impute unworthy motives to both Jewish and authoritarian churches that proclaim the right to dictate to the individual what is right and what is wrong. We may say, as many have said, that they adopt this standpoint for their own ends to acquire power and control. But that is not a satisfactory explanation, and it is an unworthy imputation. Their action is generally based on the danger of individual judgment and the peril of the individual conscience, because this privilege that we all claim does have its perils. It is so perilous, indeed, that while we pay lip service to its sanctity and sacredness, we are compelled to curtail its freedom. There is no community that can or dare base its life upon the freedom of each individual's conscience. It would result in chaos.

What is true in religion is true today in politics. Who are the happier people, those who choose their own leaders, or those who have their leaders imposed upon them? Jesus Christ does not impose Himself upon us; we choose Him, and He allows us a certain freedom. Freedom is the basis of joy. But if it oversteps the bounds of moral responsibility it is too perilous.

Individual Conscience Not a Safe Guide for Running Society as a Whole

Need I show the truth of that? Suppose every man on the street were allowed to do, unimpeded and unhindered, what he honestly believed to be right and true; what would become of modern civilization? We should be at the mercy of every moral pervert, and our standards of morality and rectitude would be meaningless and futile. We dare not allow in any community an unrestricted and an unrestrained use of the individual conscience, for the sake of our own safety. For the sake of our own moral standards and the welfare of the whole, we are compelled to maintain standards of life to which all must adjust their lives, whatever their individual consciences adjudge right. For don't imagine that every man who comes under the condemnation of a court of justice feels or believes himself to be a criminal. He doesn't. He very often has the support of his own conscience that justifies in his own eyes his criminal actions. Many of the political assassins murder their victims believing they are doing right. They are under no sense of condemnation. Their conscience justifies the deed.

We don't free ourselves from a problem of this nature by labeling them moral perverts, because you will find that that state of affairs is not confined to political assassins. In other ways, that same thing applies to respectable, law-abiding citizens. It is all a question of standards. In every community there are people whose consciences dare not be accepted as the standard for all. And you can never set up your conscience as the law for others, for who of us is perfect? And those who live by low ideals and low standards would imperil the life of the community if their standards became generally accepted.

You know, there are people today who are trying to impose their standards, what their conscience tells them is right and what is wrong, on others. That is dangerous. We are ready to acknowledge this, but for some reason fail to see that the same peril may be associated with our own conscience. Be careful lest you think that your conscience can become the standard for all people. There may lurk in your conscience and mind just as great a peril as in the conscience of the political assassin. In your zeal for making your conscience the norm for others, you are saying in effect that they have no right of private judgment. That is a point of view we must try to avoid. But it was the Lord Jesus' point of view that a man should exercise his moral faculty of judgment in matters of life and conduct.

Jesus offers to all men complete liberty of private judgment. But it is always liberty that is conditioned by an inward loyalty to revealed truth: "Search the Scriptures" and "Follow me."

THINK IT OVER

1. What was the radical teaching of Jesus about conscience that led to the charge that He was perverting the nation and leading people astray?
2. What was the position of the religionists of His day with regard to settling questions of morality and other matters of life and conduct?
3. How can freedom of conscience be abused? What are its dangers?
4. What's wrong with legalistic Christianity?
5. What attribute of character should control and direct freedom of conscience?

14

The Test of a True Conscience

A Christian is not one who is blindly obeying a rule or regulation of his church. A Christian is a person who exercises judgment and chooses to follow Jesus Christ and to do His bidding, to do what Christ would have done if He were in his place. But in advocating the right of private judgment, the Lord Jesus was also keenly aware that the peril of the low or perverted conscience was never absent. This is why He said, "Take heed," constantly watch out, "lest the light that is in thee become darkness." Be careful, that the sense of right and wrong upon which you are relying for guidance is not a blind guide.

History Records Many Great Wrongs That Were Justified by Conscience

That is the great peril of the individual conscience and it brings with it a great responsibility. The pages of history are stained with great wrongs that at one time were justified by conscience. Men have been made to pass through the fires to many a Moloch of destruction, and for precisely the same reason that the worshipers of Moloch brought this destruction upon their children, because they believed it was the right thing to do and that it was required of them. Innumerable evils have been done out of a "good" conscience. Slavery maintained its place in civilized communities for generations because conscience justified it. The horrors of the Spanish Inquisition were the outcome of a "good" conscience. Many evils today are buttressed by the individual freedom of conscience. Hands stained with blood have been declared clean by a "good" conscience. Behind almost every form of oppression that this world has known there have been the claims of a "good" conscience.

This good conscience, which is not the best or highest, has been the root from which all kinds of evils have sprung. An unenlightened sense of right and wrong has been the curse of the ages and it remains so today. That too might be the curse of your life and mine, an unenlightened conscience. We may be doing certain things, thinking that we are doing right, because our darkened conscience is approving them. It makes no difference, however, what we think is right or wrong. That cannot justify our way of living. There is a higher standard and a truer standard than our own conscience, that alone can justify our ways before God. We shall stand, not before the judgment seat of our own conscience, but before the judgment seat of Christ.

Conscience Must Be Tested by the Principles and Spirit of Christ

Not every coin that bears the true stamp is a genuine coin. Very often, the counterfeit, the base and worthless coin, bears the right stamp also. It isn't the impress that matters so much as the nature of the metal. Many an action that bears the impress of a good conscience before God is condemned as perilous, injurious, and destructive in its issues. The coin must be tested on the touchstone to discover if it rings true. And conscience must be tested on the touchstone of Christian principle and the Spirit of the Master. It is not enough to say, "It appears right to me." We must ask how does this action, this line of conduct, ring on the touchstone of Christian principle? Not what we think but what Christ thinks, what the Master thinks, matters most.

Watch Out for Influences That May Pervert the Conscience

There is nothing more essential than this, because we are all liable to be corrupted or perverted in our moral judgments by the influences that play upon our lives. The strong propensities of our nature, the prevailing atmosphere of our environment, the early training, the unchallenged habit, the thoughtless deed, the influence of other lives, the thousand and one things that bear down upon and influence the soul, all tend to create a conscience for us that may not reflect the mind of the Lord Jesus Christ. Test it on the touchstone of His great principles. We may be very sincere but we may be very wrong. We may be loyal to a conscience that is itself our condemnation. The stamp may be true but the metal base. "Take heed therefore that the light which is in thee be not darkness . . . If therefore the light that is in thee be darkness, how great is that darkness!" (Luke 11:35; Matt. 6:23). To have a guide that is blind is worse than having no guide at all. We must be careful lest our conscience becomes darkened and we are led to destruction.

Just think of how marvelously God has made the light and has put in us the ability to receive that light through our eyes. And just as the body has an eye to appropriate the outside light, the soul also has an eye that can appropriate spiritual light. Actually, the eye within us is more glorious than the light without. The intellectual part of the creation exceeds the glories of the sensible and corporeal.

The Two Faculties of the Inward Light Given to Us by God

The inward light is the ability that God has given us to make judgments, to reason out situations. Through it we collect the general truths that God has given us, and form them into propositions. And these propositions of life govern our discourse and our conduct. We see, we reason, we decide, we make choices. This is a fantastic thing that God has given us the ability to do — the faculty or power of the soul to discourse on these propositions, to speak, to explain, to reason. We can improve or diminish such propositions. We can use them or abuse them, cultivate or neglect them — and there are people doing either. Everyone is endowed with this intellectual power or faculty of the soul that the Lord Jesus calls the light within us.

Now two offices belong to this faculty. First, it informs or directs. As it informs the soul, it is called the light of nature, which is just information. And just as we have information of nature, we have information of the Spirit of God.

Secondly, this wonderful faculty of being able to collect information, to reason and to put it into propositions, has the ability to command or compel us. As it compels the soul, it's called the law of nature. The *light* of nature informs us, enables us to make propositions. The *law* of nature compels us to conform. We don't have any choice: We have to breathe. There is only one thing that we can breathe to keep us alive, and God made it that way. That's a law. But there are things that God is giving light or information about that we can choose what to do with them.

Now these two offices of informing and commanding of the light of nature and the law of nature, although belonging to the same faculty, are very different. To do, you must first be informed. To go anywhere, you must first receive light. But you are informed of much more than you have to do. You don't really use all the light that is around you. You have to choose which light you will permit to come into you. The light of nature precedes the law of nature. The light within us means the information within us, our conscience, which God has put there. The light that God has put within us involves both the faculty of information and the faculty of command, informing us and obliging us to conform.

Now conscience primarily informs; that is the proper effect of light. Conscience is both a light and a law, but it is primarily a light, not a law. It doesn't oblige or compel us, it just informs us. We do not do all that our conscience enlightens us about. We must understand the difference between the enlightening and the obliging office of our conscience.

The Light Within Is Our Conscience — God's Gift to All Mankind

Now what is the nature of the light here spoken of by our Savior? This light is certainly the great and sovereign gift of God to mankind. Even as natural light is God's physical gift to us, so is the spiritual light, conscience. It is for the guidance and government of our actions in all that concerns us with reference to this life or a better life. All our actions are motivated, are guided, by something within us, a light of God. We call it conscience.

But this conscience is also capable of being turned into darkness, our Lord tells us, and thereby made wholly useless.

We must take heed lest what can be useful light may be darkness. Extraordinary measures are needed to prevent this from happening. Since we are warned against it, it must be an evil to be avoided, otherwise the warning is superfluous.

Physical Darkness and Spiritual Darkness Make It Impossible to Make Right Choices

To understand this evil, let us consider those intolerable evils which bodily blindness, deafness, mental stupor, and an utter deprivation of all sense must unavoidably subject the outward man to. You know, spiritual truths can be learned by looking at material facts. Now blindness eliminates the possibility of choice in many areas, and spiritual blindness, the darkening of the conscience, eliminates the possibility of moral choices. If anyone seeks to take a blind and deaf person's life, the victim can neither see nor hear his approach till he finds himself actually in his murderer's hands.

Without spiritual light, without spiritual sensibility, man cannot distinguish between good and evil. You will find people drawn into doing evil all the time. They have no power to distinguish. Life and death, vice and virtue, come alike to the spiritually insensitive person, as all things are of the same color to him who cannot see. His whole soul is nothing but night and confusion, darkness and indistinction. Since he cannot see the way to happiness, how can he choose happiness? It is impossible. A blind man cannot choose his way. He has to go in the one way that he is directed; and if a person's conscience is darkened there is only one way he can go and that way is evil. He can neither see the way to destruction nor can he choose the way to heaven and therefore he cannot avoid destruction. Where there is no sense of things there can be no distinction, and where there is no distinction there can be no choice. A man destitute of this directing and distinguishing light within him is and must be at the mercy of everything in nature that would impose or serve a turn against him. Whatever the devil would have him do, that he must do. So that's the first thing that spiritual blindness does to a person; it deprives him of the ability to choose.

The danger is very great indeed. It is as frequent as it is fatal. It is sin which brings this darkness upon the soul. As we have said before, the word darkness means sin in the Scriptures. Sin blinds the eyes and then drives us headlong into perdition.

No Man Is Born without the Light of Conscience to Direct Him

What are the methods used by our enemy to deprive us of the last surviving spark of this light within us and to turn it into darkness? No man, in respect of conscience, is born blind. There is the light of God in every man to direct him, and it is the rejection of that light that brings perdition, that brings God's punishment. God would not hold anybody responsible who had not received any light. But God gives light to everyone, and everyone does something with that light. Though no man is born blind, as far as conscience is concerned, there are people who make themselves blind. No one can strike out the eye of their conscience but themselves. Therefore we cannot blame anyone else for our sinful condition. A person may love his sin so much that he plucks out his own eyes, so to speak, to give them to it. Every obstinate sinner in the world actually plucks his eyes out, deadens his conscience, makes the light that God has given originally, darkness.

Speaking of conscience, E. L. Allen said, "Honestly, what use do we make of our God-given reason? I know what use I make of it myself. I use it chiefly to provide reasons for what I want to do in pursuit of some private end I do not like to acknowledge. And a man may have his conscience so well disciplined and trained, that instead of blazing a trail before him, it is like a pet dog which just trots obediently at his heels and never so much as barks! 'If therefore the light that is in thee be darkness, how great is that darkness!' "

THINK IT OVER

1. Because your conscience tells you a thing is right, is it necessarily right in God's sight?
2. What is the true test of conscience?
3. What influences can pervert the conscience, even without our knowledge or conscious consent?
4. What quality in us willingly blinds the eye of the soul and thus darkens our conscience?

15

The Fully Illuminated Christian

In Luke 11:36 our Lord tells us, "If thy whole body therefore be full of light, having no part dark, the whole shall be full of light, as when the bright shining of a candle doth give thee light [or 'the brilliance,' actually]." Since this verse begins with "If therefore," it is the conclusion of the figurative presentation about the candle illuminating the whole body, that is, the entrance of the Lord Jesus Christ making our whole personality luminous. It rounds out the whole by carrying us back to the candle mentioned in verse 33: "No man, when he hath lighted a candle, putteth it in a secret place, neither under a bushel, but on a candlestick, that they which come in may see the light." That's the entrance of the light within us resulting in our whole body becoming luminous. The point of the whole statement is found in the last clause, "as when the lamp keeps lighting thee with brilliance."

Now in verse 34 we are pointed from the cause to the effect. The single eye makes the whole body full of light. In other words, the eye that is healthy permits the light to come into the body, and the wicked eye does not permit the light; therefore the darkness persists. Here the effect in verse 36 points us to the cause. The body's being wholly full of light is due to the brilliance of the candle. In other words, if we are full of light, it is owing to the light that has come to us from without, from the Lord Jesus Christ. An emphasis runs through the statement about the effect. The whole body is lighted up, wholly, completely. This is the positive statement. Not having any part full of darkness, that's the negative.

When Jesus Lights Our Being We Lead a Consistently Godly Life

Of course, we can be fully lighted or partially lighted. And this is matched in the last clause by the brilliance with which the candle lights us. The Greek verb here meaning "lights thee" is in the present tense, which means a continuous lighting. And Jesus lights up no mere corner of our being but fills us completely and leaves no part dark. It is complete, full illumination of our whole personality. As a result, the mouth does not confess Jesus while the hands disobey Him; the head does not bow in worship before Him while the feet walk in the counsel of the ungodly. It's a complete illumination, a complete yielding of the whole body to that light. The brilliance of the candle illumines us altogether and completely.

Now, we have a word here that in some versions is translated "brilliance." It says here, "If therefore thy whole body is full of light, not having any part full of darkness, it will be wholly lighted up, as when the lamp keeps lighting thee with brilliance." That is to say, the light that has come to us ought to be so bright that everybody can look at it and be really astonished. What this verse actually teaches is that the need in the Christian Church is a revival of godly living, that the people of the world may look at us and see how illumined we are by Jesus Christ.

It was Gladstone who said, "My only hope for the world is in bringing the human mind into contact with divine revelation through practical Christianity." The life that is possessed by God, by His light, is first of all luminous, it gives light. Therefore the candle has to be on a candlestick. For what purpose? Verse 33 gives us the answer: "that they who come in may see."

Mortal man through regeneration can suggest God to the world. The world must see something in us that cannot be explained on the basis of the purely human. No other human being could have such an influence upon us as to make us brilliant spiritually. This is what Christ meant when He said, "Ye are the light of the world." We shine with the light of Jesus Christ within us. By character and conduct we are to represent Him to the world.

Murray McCheyne, that great preacher, said, "The Christian is just a person who makes it easy for others to believe in God." Is it easy for others to believe in God because of your presence among them? And that great scientist Pascal said. "I saw that everything that came to pass in the life of Christ must be repeated in the lives of His followers." And another author said, "Say not that thou hast royal blood in thy veins, say not that thou art born of God, if thou canst not prove thy pedigree by daring to be holy."

Not Merely What We Say or Do, but What We Are, Is the Most Convincing Witness to Others

The best argument for Christianity is a consistent Christian life. There is no argument against the silent eloquence of holiness. You know, a lighthouse building would be dangerous but for the light it sheds abroad, and so it is with us. We may be lighthouses without light. Ships can break themselves on the

135

rock. It is not merely what we say, nor what we do, but what we are that matters. That is the witness that is convincing. The greatest thing about us is often our unconscious influence. II Corinthians 4:11 says, "that the life also of Jesus might be made manifest in our mortal flesh." "Manifest" is the same word, "brilliantly seen," that we have mentioned before. We accomplish more by our radiations than by our exhortations. May God make us luminous Christians. That's what the light of Christ does for us.

Have you ever put a candle within an alabaster vase? I've seen this many times in Egypt; in fact, I have brought some vases back with me from time to time. I have an onyx vase, for instance, from Ephesus, in Turkey, that, when a light is put inside the whole thing becomes luminous. That's exactly what happens when Jesus Christ comes into our hearts. We become bright, luminous. Other people can find their way to God through the light we shed abroad.

Luminous and Transparent Christians

The life that is enlightened by Christ is also a life that is transparent, having no part dark. That is the best definition, really, of full salvation. And that's the kind of salvation Jesus Christ gives us. We read in Psalm 51:6, "Behold, thou desirest truth in the inward parts: and in the hidden part thou shalt make me to know wisdom." The great work of the Holy Spirit is in the deep regions of our personality, which can only be illumined by the light of God. Every part of our personality must come under that searching light. Within the range of that light, surely there can be no part dark.

Are there regions of your life that are not transparent? It is a wrong concept of the Christian life, that it is an imitation instead of a participation. We don't imitate Christ, we participate in His life. We allow His light to come into our hearts, and that's what shines. Symbolically speaking, He makes our whole body luminous and transparent, so that we are able to show to the world the Christ that is within us. Christ is seen through us. We are in Christ and He is in us.

What the light reveals, the precious blood of Christ can heal. Some men are experts at pruning, but the Savior can deal with both root and branch. Paul says in Romans 8:2, "the law of the Spirit of life in Christ Jesus hath made me free from the law of sin and death." He has made us free. This is something deeper than mere counteraction or suppression. He's a Savior who can save from all sin.

> Holiness by faith in Jesus,
> Not by effort of thine own;
> Sin's dominion crushed and broken
> By the power of grace alone.

The Need of a Personal Assurance from God of Our Salvation

This is surely where we realize the wonder of God's saving grace. A truth we do not always take to heart is that, in sanctification as well as in regeneration, God must speak to us in His own voice. When face to face with our desperate need we read salvation promises such as John 1:12 and I John 1:9: "But as many as received him, to them gave he power to become the sons of God, even to them that believe on his name . . . If we confess our sins, he is faithful and just to forgive us our sins, and to cleanse us from all unrighteousness." But the words we read on paper must be implanted in our consciousness, they must be spoken into us by the power of the Holy Spirit. No honest soul will be satisfied with a dead, legal imputation of holiness. Nothing short of God revealing Himself in us and speaking His word of deliverance and assurance will answer to our deep needs.

137

Someone has said, "The Redeemer who loved us from eternity and formed us for Himself will not leave the pining soul to the secondhand tinkering of others. He will closet us in with Himself." I believe God longs to give to each of us a perfect personal assurance of His perfect salvation. Yet how few seem to realize this, as David Brainerd did. In his diary he wrote: "My discourse was suited to my own case, for of late I have found a great want of apprehension of divine grace and have often been greatly distressed in my soul because I did not suitably apprehend this fountain open to purge away sin, and so I've had to be laboring for spiritual life and peace of conscience in my own strength; but now God showed me in some measure the arm of strength and fountain of all grace. But do I hear someone say, can He meet me at the point of my need? Let me tell you that He absolutely can."

Deliverance from Sin's Condemnation and Power through the Cross of Christ

There are those today in the Christian Church who have tried every move to make a success of their Christian profession, but they have failed, and failed utterly. May I say that the voice of Christ comes ringing over the field of our defeat, our ways of frustration and baffling, with this cry of assurance, "I can save you yet." God has an answer to every checkmate in life. Did I not believe this, I would never stand on the doctrine that God can cleanse our lives, our bodies completely. Holiness is not human life brought up to the highest level of development, but divine life brought down to the lowest level of condescension. We must ever remember that the cross is not only the fundamental basis in the sinner's conversion but also the fundamental instrument in the believer's sanctification. The one aspect brings deliverance from sin's condemnation, but the other from sin's power, so

138

that we proclaim victory through the blood.

The Call to a Sacrificial Life

And in the third place this life of illumination by Christ is a light that is burning. It speaks of vision and passion, but never forget that the light that glows burns on the altar of sacrifice. Let us not forget that the cross that called Jesus to a sacrificial death calls His disciples to a sacrificial life.

How does your life measure up? Is it luminous? Is it transparent? Is it burning for Christ? Is it sacrificial? Is His light burning within you so that the brilliance of your entire personality shows forth the light of Christ to others? Do not hide it. Let the light of Jesus shine in and through you completely.

> Have Thine own way, Lord,
> Have Thine own way;
> Hold o'er my being
> Absolute sway.
> Fill with Thy Spirit
> Till all shall see
> Christ only, always,
> Living in me!
> — Adelaide A. Pollard

THINK IT OVER

1. What is the best evidence of a fully illuminated heart? (Hint: read Luke 6:46.)
2. What is the most convincing witness to others:
   a. What we say?

b. What we do?

c. What we are?

3. Read the last two paragraphs of this chapter over, and answer the questions honestly to find where you stand as a "light-bearer." May the closing poem be your prayer and mine as we seek together to "shine for Jesus."

I

INDEX OF SUBJECTS

(For fuller index see Index of Greek Words)

II

INDEX OF ENGLISH WORDS

III

INDEX OF GREEK WORDS

IV

INDEX OF SCRIPTURES

V

ILLUSTRATION INDEX